The story of Ida Pfeiffer and her travels in many lands

Anonymous

Alpha Editions

This edition published in 2024

ISBN : 9789362920683

Design and Setting By
Alpha Editions
www.alphaedis.com
Email - info@alphaedis.com

As per information held with us this book is in Public Domain.
This book is a reproduction of an important historical work. Alpha Editions uses the best technology to reproduce historical work in the same manner it was first published to preserve its original nature. Any marks or number seen are left intentionally to preserve its true form.

Contents

CHAPTER I.—HER BIOGRAPHY..- 1 -

CHAPTER II.—JOURNEY ROUND THE WORLD. ....- 9 -

CHAPTER III.—NORTHWARD. ....- 47 -

CHAPTER IV.—LAST TRAVELS. ....- 68 -

NOTES..- 79 -

CHAPTER I.—HER BIOGRAPHY.

Ida Pfeiffer, the celebrated traveller, was born in Vienna on the 14th of October 1797. She was the third child of a well-to-do merchant, named Reyer; and at an early age gave indications of an original and self-possessed character. The only girl in a family of six children, her predilections were favoured by the circumstances which surrounded her. She was bold, enterprising, fond of sport and exercise; loved to dress like her brothers, and to share in their escapades. Dolls she contemptuously put aside, preferring drums; and a sword or a gun was valued at much more than a doll's house. In some respects her father brought her up strictly; she was fed, like her brothers, on a simple and even meagre diet, and trained to habits of prompt obedience; but he did nothing to discourage her taste for more violent exercises than are commonly permitted to young girls.

She was only in her tenth year, however, when he died; and she then passed naturally enough under the maternal control. Between her own inclinations and her mother's ideas of maidenly culture a great contest immediately arose. Her mother could not understand why her daughter should prefer the violin to the piano, and the masculine trousers to the feminine petticoat. In fact, she did not understand Ida, and it may be assumed that Ida did not understand her.

In 1809 Vienna was captured by the French army under Napoleon; a disgrace which the brave and spirited Ida felt most keenly. Some of the victorious troops were quartered in the house of her mother, who thought it politic to treat them with courtesy; but her daughter neither could nor would repress her dislike. When compelled to be present at a grand review which Napoleon held in Schönbrunn, she turned her back as the emperor rode past. For this hazardous manœuvre she was summarily punished; and to prevent her from repeating it when the emperor returned, her mother held her by the shoulders. This was of little avail, however, as Ida perseveringly persisted in keeping her eyes shut.

At the age of thirteen she was induced to resume the garb of her sex, though it was some time before she could accustom her wild free movements to it. She was then placed in charge of a tutor, who seems to have behaved to her with equal skill and delicacy. "He showed," she says, "great patience and perseverance in combating my overstrained and misdirected notions. As I had learned to fear my parents rather than love them, and this gentleman was, so to speak, the first human being who had displayed any sympathy and affection for me, I clung to him in return with enthusiastic attachment, desirous of fulfilling his every wish, and never so happy as when he appeared satisfied with my exertions. He took the entire charge of my education, and though it cost me some tears to abandon my youthful visions, and engage in pursuits I had hitherto regarded with contempt, to all this I submitted out of my affection for him. I even learned many feminine avocations, such as sewing, knitting, and cookery. To him I owed the insight I obtained into the duties and true position of my sex; and it was he who transformed me from a romp and a hoyden into a modest quiet girl."

Already a great longing for travel had entered into her mind. She longed to see new scenes, new peoples, new manners and customs. She read eagerly every book of travel that fell into her hands; followed with profound interest the career of every adventurous explorer, and blamed her sex that prevented her from following their heroic examples. For a while a change was effected in the current of her thoughts by a strong attachment which sprung up between her and her teacher, who by this time had given up his former profession, and had obtained an honourable position in the civil service. It was natural enough that in the close intimacy which existed between them such an affection should be developed. Ida's mother, however, regarded it with grave disapproval, and exacted from the unfortunate girl a promise that she would neither see nor write to her humble suitor again. The result was a dangerous illness: on her recovery from which her mother insisted on her accepting for a husband Dr. Pfeiffer, a widower, with a grown-up son, but an opulent and distinguished advocate in Lemberg, who was then on a visit to Vienna. Though twenty-four years older than Ida, he was attracted by her grace and simplicity, and offered his hand. Weary of home persecutions, Ida accepted it, and the marriage took place on May 1st, 1820.

If she did not love her husband, she respected him, and their married life was not unhappy. In a few months, however, her husband's integrity led to a sad change of fortune. He had fully and fearlessly exposed the corruption of the Austrian officials in Galicia, and had thus made many enemies. He was compelled to give up his office as councillor, and, deprived of his lucrative practice, to remove to Vienna in search of employment. Through the treachery of a friend, Ida's fortune was lost, and the ill-fated couple found themselves reduced to the most painful exigencies. Vienna, Lemberg, Vienna again, Switzerland, everywhere Dr. Pfeiffer sought work, and everywhere found himself baffled by some malignant influence. "Heaven only knows," says Madame Pfeiffer in her autobiography, "what I suffered during eighteen years of my married life; not, indeed, from any ill-treatment on my husband's part, but from poverty and want. I came of a wealthy family, and had been accustomed from my earliest youth to order and comfort; and now I frequently knew not where I should lay my head, or find a little money to buy the commonest necessaries. I performed household drudgery, and endured cold and hunger; I worked secretly for money, and gave lessons in drawing and music; and yet, in spite of all my exertions, there were many days when I could hardly put anything but dry bread before my poor children for their dinner." These children were two sons, whose education their mother entirely undertook, until, after old Madame Reyer's death in 1837, she succeeded to an inheritance, which lifted the little family out of the slough of poverty, and enabled her to provide her sons with good teachers.

As they grew up and engaged successfully in professional pursuits, Madame Pfeiffer, who had lost her husband in 1838, found herself once more under the spell of her old passion for travel, and in a position to gratify her adventurous inclinations. Her means were somewhat limited, it is true, for she had done much for her husband and her children; but economy was natural to her, and she retained the simple habits she had acquired in her childhood. She was strong, healthy, courageous, and accomplished; and at length, after maturing her plans with anxious consideration, she took up her pilgrim's staff, and sallied forth alone.

Her first object was to visit the Holy Land, and tread in the hallowed footsteps of our Lord. For this purpose she left Vienna on the 22nd of March 1842, and embarked on board the steamer that was to convey her down the Danube to the Black Sea and the city of Constantinople. Thence she repaired to Broussa, Beirut, Jaffa, Jerusalem, the Dead Sea, Nazareth, Damascus, Baalbek, the Lebanon, Alexandria, and Cairo; and travelled across the sandy Desert to the Isthmus of Suez and the Red Sea. From Egypt the adventurous lady returned home by way of Sicily and Italy, visiting Naples, Rome, and Florence, and arriving in Vienna in December 1842. In the following year she published the record of her experiences under the title of a "Journey of a Viennese Lady to the Holy Land." It met with a very favourable reception, to which the simplicity of its style and the faithfulness of its descriptions fully entitled it.

With the profits of this book to swell her funds, Madame Pfeiffer felt emboldened to undertake a new expedition; and this time she resolved on a northern pilgrimage, expecting in *Ultima Thule* to see nature manifested on a novel and surprising scale. She began her journey to Iceland on the 10th of April 1845, and returned to Vienna on the 4th of October. Her narrative of this second voyage will be found, necessarily much abridged and condensed, in the following pages.

What should she do next? Success had increased her courage and strengthened her resolution, and she could think of nothing fit for her energies and sufficient for her curiosity but a voyage round the world! She argued that greater privations and fatigue than she had endured in Syria and Iceland she could scarcely be called upon to encounter. The outlay did not frighten her; for she had learned by experience how little is required, if the traveller will but practise the strictest economy and resolutely forego many comforts and all superfluities. Her savings amounted to a sum insufficient, perhaps, for such travellers as Prince Pückler-Muskau, Chateaubriand, or Lamartine for a fortnight's excursion; but for a woman who wanted to see much, but cared for no personal indulgence, it seemed enough to last during a journey of two or three years. And so it proved.

The heroic woman set out alone on the 1st of May 1846, and proceeded first to Rio Janeiro. On the 3rd of February 1847, she sailed round Cape Horn, and on the 2nd of March landed at Valparaiso. Thence she traversed the broad Pacific to Tahiti, where she was presented to Queen Pomare. In the beginning of July we find her at Macao; afterwards she visited Hong Kong and Canton, where the appearance of a white woman produced a remarkable and rather disagreeable sensation. By way of Singapore she proceeded to Ceylon, which she carefully explored, making excursions to Colombo, Candy, and the famous temple of Dagoba. Towards the end of October she landed at Madras, and thence went on to Calcutta, ascending the Ganges to the holy city of Benares, and striking across the country to Bombay. Late in the month of April 1848 she sailed for Persia, and from Bushire traversed the interior as far as legend-haunted Bagdad. After a pilgrimage to the ruins of Ctesiphon and Babylon, this bold lady accompanied a caravan through the dreary desert to Mosul and the vast ruins of Nineveh, and afterwards to the salt lake of Urumiyeh and the city of Tabreez. It is certain that no woman ever accomplished a more daring exploit! The mental as well as physical energy required was enormous; and only a strong mind and a strong frame could have endured the many hardships consequent on her undertaking—the burning heat by day, the inconveniences of every kind at night, the perils incidental to her sex, meagre fare, a filthy couch, and constant apprehension of attack by robber bands. The English consul at Tabreez, when she introduced herself to him, found it hard to believe that a woman could have accomplished such an enterprise.

At Tabreez, Madame Pfeiffer was presented to the Viceroy, and obtained permission to visit his harem. On August 11th, 1848, she resumed her journey, crossing Armenia, Georgia, and Mingrelia; she touched afterwards at Anapa, Kertch, and Sebastopol, landed at Odessa, and returned home by way of Constantinople, Greece, the Ionian Islands, and Trieste, arriving in Vienna on the 4th of November 1848, just after the city had been recaptured from the rebels by the troops of Prince Windischgrätz.

Ida Pfeiffer was now a woman of note. Her name was known in every civilized country; and it was not unnatural that great celebrity should attach to a female who, alone, and without the protection of rank or official recommendation, had travelled 2800 miles by land, and 35,000 miles by sea. Hence, her next work, "A Woman's Journey Round the World," was most favourably received, and translated both into French and English. A summary of it is included in our little volume.

The brave adventurer at first, on her return home, spoke of her travelling days as over, and, at the age of fifty-four, as desirous of peace and rest. But this tranquil frame of mind was of very brief duration. Her love of action and thirst of novelty could not long be repressed; and as she felt herself still strong and healthy, with energies as quick and lively as ever, she resolved on a second circuit of the globe. Her funds having been increased by a grant of 1500 florins from the Austrian Government, she left Vienna on the 18th of March 1851, proceeded to London, and thence to Cape Town, where she arrived on the 11th of August. For a while she hesitated between a visit to the interior of Africa and a voyage to Australia; but at last she sailed to Singapore, and determined to explore the East Indian Archipelago. At Sarawak, the British settlement in Borneo, she was warmly welcomed by Sir James Brooke, a man of heroic temper and unusual capacities for command and organization. She adventured among the Dyaks, and journeyed westward to Pontianak, and the diamond mines of Landak. We next meet with her in Java, and afterwards in Sumatra, where she boldly trusted herself among the cannibal Battas, who had hitherto resented the intrusion of any European. Returning to Java, she saw almost all that it had of natural wonders or natural beauties; and then departed on a tour through the Sunda Islands and the Moluccas, visiting Banda, Amboyna, Ceram, Ternate, and Celebes.

For a second time she traversed the Pacific, but on this occasion in an opposite direction. For two months she saw no land; but on the 27th September 1853 she arrived at San Francisco. At the close of the year she sailed for Callao. Thence she repaired to Lima, with the intention of crossing the Andes, and pushing eastward, through the interior of South America, to the Brazilian coast. A revolution in Peru, however, compelled her to change her course, and she returned to Ecuador, which served as a starting-point for her ascent of the Cordilleras. After having the good fortune to witness an eruption of Cotopaxi, she retraced her steps to the west. In the neighbourhood of Guayaquil she had two very narrow escapes: one, by a fall from her mule; and next, by an immersion in the River Guaya, which teems with alligators. Meeting with neither courtesy nor help from the Spanish Americans—a superstitious, ignorant, and degraded race—she gladly set sail for Panama.

At the end of May she crossed the Isthmus, and sailed to New Orleans. Thence she ascended the Mississippi to Napoleon, and the Arkansas to Fort Smith. After suffering from a severe attack of fever, she made her way to St. Louis, and then directed her steps northward to St. Paul, the Falls of St. Antony, Chicago, and thence to the great Lakes and "mighty Niagara." After an excursion into Canada, she visited New York, Boston, and other great cities, crossed the Atlantic, and arrived in England on the 21st of November 1854. Two years later she published a narrative of her adventures, entitled "My Second Journey Round the World."

Madame Pfeiffer's last voyage was to Madagascar, and will be found described in the closing chapter of this little volume. In Madagascar she contracted a dangerous illness, from which she temporarily recovered; but on her return to Europe it was evident that her constitution had received a severe blow. She gradually grew weaker. Her disease proved to be cancer of the liver, and the physicians pronounced it incurable. After lingering a few weeks in much pain, she passed away on the night of the 27th of October 1858, in the sixty-third year of her age.

* * * * *

This remarkable woman is described as of short stature, thin, and slightly bent. Her movements were deliberate and measured. She was well-knit and of considerable physical energy, and her career proves her to have been possessed of no ordinary powers of endurance. The reader might probably suppose that she was what is commonly known as a strong-minded woman. The epithet would suit her if seriously applied, for she had undoubtedly a clear, strong intellect, a cool judgment, and a resolute purpose; but it would be thoroughly inapplicable in the satirical sense in which it is commonly used. There was nothing masculine about her. On the contrary, she was so reserved and so unassuming that it required an intimate knowledge of her to fathom the depths of her acquirements and experience. "In her whole appearance and manner," we are told, "was a staidness that seemed to indicate the practical housewife, with no thought soaring beyond her domestic concerns."

This quiet, silent woman, travelled nearly 20,000 miles by land and 150,000 miles by sea; visiting regions which no European had previously penetrated, or where the bravest men had found it difficult to make their way; undergoing a variety of severe experiences; opening up numerous novel and surprising scenes; and doing all this with the scantiest means, and unassisted by powerful protection or royal patronage. We doubt whether the entire round of human enterprise presents anything more remarkable or more admirable. And it would be unfair to suppose that she was actuated only by a feminine curiosity. Her leading motive was a thirst for knowledge. At all events, if she had a passion for travelling, it must be admitted that her qualifications as a traveller were unusual. Her observation was quick and accurate; her perseverance was indefatigable; her courage never faltered; while she possessed a peculiar talent for first awakening, and then profiting by, the interest and sympathy of those with whom she came in contact.

To assert that her travels were wholly without scientific value would be unjust; Humboldt and Carl Ritter were of a different opinion. She made her way into regions which had never before been trodden by European foot; and the very fact of her sex was a frequent protection in her most dangerous undertakings. She was allowed to enter many places which would have been rigorously barred against male travellers. Consequently, her communications have the merit of embodying many new facts in geography and ethnology, and of correcting numerous popular errors.

Science derived much benefit also from her valuable collections of plants, animals, and minerals.

We conclude with the eulogium pronounced by an anonymous biographer:—"Straightforward in character, and endued with high principle, she possessed, moreover, a wisdom and a promptitude in action seldom equalled among her sex. Ida Pfeiffer may, indeed, justly be classed among those women who richly compensate for the absence of outward charms by their remarkable energy and the rare qualities of their minds."

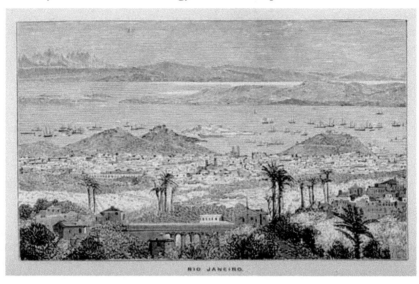
RIO JANEIRO.

CHAPTER II.—JOURNEY ROUND THE WORLD.

Prompted by a boundless thirst for knowledge and an insatiable desire to see new places and new things, Madame Pfeiffer left Vienna on the 1st of May 1846, and proceeded to Hamburg, where she embarked on board a Danish brig, the *Caroline*, for Rio Janeiro. As the voyage was divested of romantic incidents, we shall land the reader without delay at the great seaport of the Brazilian empire.

The traveller's description of it is not very favourably coloured. The streets are dirty, and the houses, even the public buildings, insignificant. The Imperial Palace has not the slightest architectural pretensions. The finest square is the Largo do Roico, but this would not be admitted into Belgravia. It is impossible to speak in high terms even of the churches, the interior of which is not less disappointing than their exterior. And as is the town, so are the inhabitants. Negroes and mulattoes do not make up attractive pictures. Some of the Brazilian and Portuguese women, however, have handsome and expressive countenances.

Most writers indulge in glowing descriptions of the scenery and climate of the Brazils; of the cloudless, radiant sky, and the magic of the never-ending spring. Madame Ida Pfeiffer admits that the vegetation is richer, and the soil more fruitful, and nature more exuberantly active than in any other part of the world; but still, she says, it must not be thought that all is good and beautiful, and that there is nothing to weaken the powerful effect of the first impression. The constant blaze of colour after a while begins to weary; the eye wants rest; the monotony of the verdure oppresses; and we begin to understand that the true loveliness of spring is only rightly appreciated when it succeeds the harsher aspects of winter.

INVASION OF ANTS.

Europeans suffer much from the climate. The moisture is very considerable, and renders the heat, which in the hot months rises to 99° in the shade, and 122° in the sun, more difficult to bear. Fogs and mists are disagreeably common; and whole tracts of country are often veiled by an impenetrable mist.

The Brazils suffer, too, from a plague of insects,—from mosquitoes, ants, baraten, and sand-fleas; against the attacks of which the traveller finds it difficult to defend himself. The ants often appear in trains of immeasurable length, and pursue their march over every obstacle that stands in the way. Madame Pfeiffer, during her residence at a friend's house, beheld the advance of a swarm of this description. It was really interesting to see what a regular line they formed; nothing could make them deviate from the direction on which they had first determined. Madame Geiger, her friend, told her she was awakened one night by a terrible itching: she sprang out of bed immediately, and lo, a swarm of ants were passing over it! There is no remedy for the infliction, except to wait, with as much patience as one can muster, for the end of the procession, which frequently lasts four to six hours. It is possible, to some extent, to protect provisions against their attacks, by placing the legs of the tables in basins filled with water. Clothes and linen are enclosed in tightly-fitting tin canisters.

The worst plague of all, however, are the sand-fleas, which attach themselves to one's toes, underneath the nail, or sometimes to the soles of the feet. When a person feels an irritation in these parts, he must immediately look at the place; and if he discern a tiny black point, surrounded by a small white ring, the former is the *chigoe*, or sand-flea, and the latter the eggs which it has deposited in the flesh. The first thing to be done is to loosen the skin all round as far as the white skin is visible; the whole deposit is then extracted, and a little snuff strewn in the empty space. The blacks perform this operation with considerable skill.

Rich as the Brazils are in natural productions, they are wanting in many articles which Europeans regard as of the first importance. There are sugar and coffee, it is true; but no corn, no potatoes, and none of our delightful varieties of fruit. The flour of manioc, obtained from the cassava plant, which forms a staple portion of almost every dish, supplies the place of bread, but is far from being so nutritious and strengthening; while the different kinds of sweet-tasting roots are far inferior in value to our potato. The only fruit which Madame Pfeiffer thought really excellent, were the oranges, bananas, and mangoes. The pine-apples are neither very sweet nor very fragrant. And with regard to two most important articles of consumption, the milk is very watery, and the meat very dry.

* * * * *

Our traveller, during her sojourn at Rio Janeiro, made many interesting excursions in the neighbourhood. One was directed to Petropolis, a colony founded by Germans in the heart of scenery of the most exquisite character. Accompanied by Count Berchthold, she sailed for Porto d'Estrella in one of the regular coasting barks. Their course carried them across a bay remarkable for its picturesque views. It lies calmly in the embrace of richly-wooded hills, and is studded with islands, like a silver shield with emerald bosses. Some of these islands are completely overgrown with palms, while others are masses of huge rock, with a carpet of green turf.

Their bark was manned by four negroes and a white skipper. At first they ran merrily before a favourable wind, but in two hours the crew were compelled to take to the oars, the method of using which was exceedingly fatiguing. At each dip of the oar, the rower mounts upon a bench in front of him, and then, during the stroke, throws himself off again, with his full force. In two hours more they passed into the river Geromerino, and made their way through a world of beautiful aquatic plants which covered the tranquil waters in every direction. The river banks are flat, and fringed with underwood and young trees; the background is formed by ranges of low green hills.

At Porto d'Estrella, Madame Pfeiffer and her companion landed, and proceeded on foot towards Petropolis. The first eight miles lay through a broad valley, clothed with dense brambles and young trees, and shadowed by lofty mountains. The wild pine-apples by the roadside were very fair to see; they were not quite ripe, but tinted of the most delicate red. Beautiful humming-birds flashed through the air like "winged jewels," and studded the dense foliage with points of many-coloured light.

After passing through the valley, they reached the Sierra, as the Brazilians term the practicable mountain-summits. It was three thousand feet in height, and was ascended by a broad paved road, striking through the depths of virgin forests.

Madame Pfeiffer had always imagined that the trees in virgin forests had very thick and lofty trunks; but such was not the case here; probably because the vegetation was too luxuriant, and the larger trunks have the life crushed out of them by masses of smaller trees, bushes, creepers, and parasites.

Frequent truppas, or teams of ten mules driven by a negro, as well as numerous pedestrians, enlivened the path, and prevented our travellers from observing that their steps were persistently followed up by a negro. When, however, they arrived at a somewhat lonely spot, this negro suddenly sprang forward, holding a lasso in one hand and a long knife in the other, and with threatening gestures gave them to understand that he intended to murder them, and then drag their dead bodies into the forest!

The travellers were without arms, having been told the road was perfectly safe; their only weapons were their umbrellas, with the exception of a clasp-knife. This the brave woman drew from her pocket and opened, in the calm resolution to sell her life as dearly as possible. With their umbrellas they parried their adversary's blows as long as they could; but he caught hold of Madame Ida's, which snapped off, leaving only a piece of the handle in her hand. In the struggle, however, he dropped his knife, which rolled a few steps away from him. Madame Ida immediately made a dash at it, and thought she had secured it; but, quicker in his movements than she was, he thrust her away with his hands and feet, and once more obtained possession of it. Waving it furiously over his head, he slashed her twice in the upper part of the left arm. All seemed lost; but in her extreme peril the brave lady bethought her of her own knife, and struck at her adversary, wounding him in the hand. At the same moment Count Berchthold sprang forward, and while he seized the villain with both arms, Madame Ida Pfeiffer recovered her feet. All this took place in less than a minute. The negro was now roused into a condition of maniacal fury; he gnashed his teeth like a wild beast, and brandished his knife, while uttering fearful threats. The issue of the contest would probably have been disastrous, but for the opportune arrival of assistance. Hearing the tramp of horses' hoofs upon the road, the negro desisted from his attack, and sprang into the forest. A couple of horsemen turning the corner of the road, our travellers hurried to meet them; and having told their tale, which, indeed, their wounds told eloquently enough, they leaped from their horses, and entered the wood in pursuit. A couple of negroes soon afterwards coming up, the villain was captured, securely pinioned, and, as he would not walk, severely beaten, until, as most of the blows fell upon his head, Madame Ida Pfeiffer feared that the wretch's skull would be broken. Nothing, however, would induce him to walk, and the negroes were compelled to carry him bodily, to the nearest house.

The colony of Petropolis proved to be situated in the depth of a virgin forest, at an elevation of 2500 feet above the sea-level. At the time of Madame Pfeiffer's visit it was about fourteen months old, having been founded for the special purpose of providing the capital with fruits and vegetables which, in tropical climates, will thrive only in very elevated situations. It was, of course, in a very rudimentary condition, the mere embryo of a town; but the country around it was very picturesque.

* * * * *

Madame Pfeiffer's second excursion was into the interior; and it opened up to her a variety of interesting scenes,—as, for instance, a manioc-fazenda, or plantation. The manioc plant, it appears, throws off stalks from four to six feet in height, with a number of large leaves at their upper extremities. The valuable portion of the plant is its bulbous root, which frequently weighs two or three pounds, and supplies the place of corn throughout the Brazils. It is washed, peeled, and held against the rough edge of a millstone, until it is completely ground into flour. This flour is collected in a basket, steeped thoroughly in water, and afterwards pressed quite dry by means of a press. Lastly, it is scattered upon large iron plates, and slowly dried over a gentle fire. At this stage it resembles a very coarse kind of flour, and is eaten in two ways;—either mixed with hot water, until it forms a kind of porridge; or baked in the form of coarse flour, which is handed round at table in little baskets.

She also saw a coffee plantation. The coffee-trees stand in rows upon tolerably steep hillocks. Their height ranges from six feet to twelve; and they begin to bear sometimes as early as the second, but in no case later than the third year. They are productive for at least ten years. The leaf is long and slightly serrated, and the flower white; while the fruit hangs down like a cluster of grapes, and resembles a large cherry, which varies from green to red, then to brown, and almost black. While red, the outer shell is soft; but eventually it becomes perfectly hard, until it may be compared to a wooden capsule. Blossoms and ripe fruit are found on the same tree at the same time; so that a crop may be gathered at almost any season of the year. After the berries are plucked, they are spread out in spacious areas enclosed by a wall about twelve feet high, with small drains to carry off the rain-water. Here the coffee is allowed to dry in the heat of the sun, and it is then shaken into large stone mortars, where it is lightly pounded with wooden hammers, set in motion by water power. The whole mass falls into wooden boxes attached to a long table, at which sit the negro workers, who separate the coffee from the husk, and put it into flat copper pans. In these it is carefully and skilfully turned about over a slow fire, until desiccation is complete. On the whole, says Madame Ida Pfeiffer, the preparation of the coffee is not laborious, and the harvest much more easily gathered than one of corn. The negro, while plucking the coffee, stands erect, and the tree protects him from the heat of the sun. His only danger is from poisonous snakes, and a sting from one of these is a very rare occurrence.

Another novelty which much impressed our traveller was the sight of the frequent burning forests. These are set on fire in order to clear the ground for cultivation. In most cases she viewed the tremendous spectacle from a distance; but one day she realized it in all its details, as her road lay between a wood in flames on the one hand, and the brushwood, crackling and seething, on the other. The space between the double rows of fire did not exceed fifty paces in breadth, and was completely buried in smoke. The spluttering and hissing of the fire was distinctly audible, and through the dense mass of vapour shot upward thick shafts and tongues of flame, while now and then the large trees crashed to the ground, with loud reports, like those of artillery.

A FOREST ON FIRE.

"On seeing my guide enter this fiery gulf," says our traveller, "I was, I must confess, rather frightened;" and her dread was surely very excusable. She plucked up courage, however, when she saw that her guide pushed forward. On the threshold, so to speak, sat two negroes, to indicate the safe, and, in truth, the only path. The guide, in obedience to their warning, spurred on his mule, and, followed by Madame Pfeiffer, galloped at full speed across the desert of fire. Flames to the right of them, flames to the left of them, onward they dashed, and happily effected the passage in safety.

* * * * *

Madame Pfeiffer gives a bright description of the beauties of the road as she pushed further into the interior. Crossing a small waterfall, she struck right into the depths of the virgin forest, pursuing a narrow path which ran along the bank of a little stream. Palms, with their lordly crests, soared high above the other trees, which, intertwined by inextricable boughs, formed the loveliest fairy-bowers imaginable; every stem, every branch was luxuriously festooned with fantastic orchids; while creepers and ferns glided up the tall, smooth trunks, mingling with the boughs, and hanging in every direction waving curtains of flowers, of the sweetest odours and the most vivid colours. With shrill twittering cry and rapid wings flashed the humming-bird from bough to bough; the pepper-pecker, with glowing plumage, soared timorously upwards; while parrots and paroquets, and innumerable birds of beautiful appearance, added, by their cries and motions, to the liveliness of the scene.

Madame Pfeiffer visited an Indian village. It lay deep in the forest recesses, and consisted of five huts, or rather sheds, formed of leaves, and measuring eighteen feet by twelve feet, erected under lofty trees. The frames were formed of four poles stuck in the ground, with another reaching across; and the roof was wrought of palm-leaves, by no means impervious to the rain. The sides were open. In the interior hung a hammock or two; and on the earth a few roots, Indian corn, and bananas were roasting under a heap of ashes. In one corner, under the roof, a small supply of provisions was hoarded up, and round about were scattered a few gourds; these are used by the Puris as substitutes for "crockery." Their weapons, the long bows and arrows, leaned against the wall.

Madame Pfeiffer describes the Puri Indians as even uglier than the negroes. Their complexion is a light bronze; they are stunted in stature, well-knit, and about the middle size. Their features are broad and somewhat compressed; their hair is thick, long, and of a coal-black colour. The men wear it hanging straight down; the women, in plaits fastened to the back of the head, and sometimes falling loosely down about their persons. Their forehead is broad and low, and the nose somewhat flattened; the eyes are long and narrow, almost like those of the Chinese; and the mouth is large, with rather thick lips. To enhance the effect of these various charms, the countenance bears a peculiar look of stupidity, which may be attributed perhaps to the way in which the mouth is kept always open. Women, as well as males, are generally tattooed of a reddish or blue colour, round the mouth, moustachio-wise. Both sexes are addicted to smoking, and look upon brandy as the *summum bonum* of human life.

The Indians, ugly as they were, gave Madame Pfeiffer a hospitable welcome. After an evening meal, in which roasted monkey and parrot were the chief dishes, they performed one of their characteristic dances. A quantity of wood was heaped up into a funeral pile, and set on fire; the men then danced around it in a ring. They threw their bodies from side to side with much awkwardness, but always moving the head forward in a straight line. The women then joined in, forming at a short distance behind the men, and imitating all their movements. A horrible noise arose; this was intended for a song, the singers at the same time distorting their features frightfully. One of them performed on a kind of stringed instrument, made out of the stem of a cabbage-palm, and about two feet, or two feet and a half, in length. A hole was cut in it slantwise, and six fibres of the stem were kept up in an elevated position at each end, by means of a small bridge. The fingers played upon these as upon a guitar, drawing forth a very low, harsh, and disagreeable tone. The dance, thus pleasingly accompanied, was called the Dance of Peace and Joy.

A wilder measure was next undertaken by the men alone. They first equipped themselves with bows, arrows, and stout clubs; then they formed a circle, indulged in the most rapid and fantastic movements, and brandished their clubs as if dealing death to a hundred foes. Suddenly they broke their ranks, strung their bows, placed their arrows ready, and represented all the evolutions of shooting after a flying foe, giving utterance to the most piercing cries, which resounded through the forest-glades. Madame Pfeiffer, believing that she was really surrounded by enemies, started up in terror, and was heartily glad when the dance ended.

CAPE HORN.

From Rio Janeiro Madame Pfeiffer sailed in an English ship, the *John Renwick*, on the 9th of December, bound for Valparaiso in Chili. She kept to the south, touching at Santos, where the voyagers celebrated New-Year's Day, and reaching the mouth of the Rio Plata on the 11th of January. In these latitudes the Southern Cross is the most conspicuous object in the heavens. It consists of four stars of much brilliancy, arranged in two diagonal rows. Late in the month the voyagers sighted the sterile shores and barren mountains of Patagonia, and next the volcanic rocks, wave-worn and wind-worn, of Tierra del Fuego. Through the Strait of Le Maire, which separates the latter from Staten Island, they sailed onward to the extreme southern point of the American continent, the famous promontory of Cape Horn. It is the termination of the mighty mountain-chain of the Andes, and is formed of a mass of colossal basaltic rocks, thrown together in wild disorder, as by a Titan's hand.

Rounding Cape Horn they encountered a violent gale, which lasted for several days; and soon discovered, like other voyagers, how little the great southern ocean deserves its name of the Pacific. But they reached Valparaiso in safety. Its appearance, however, did not very favourably impress Madame Ida Pfeiffer. It is laid out in two long streets at the foot of dreary hills, these hills consisting of a pile of rocks covered with thin strata of earth and sand. Some of them are covered with houses; on one of them is the churchyard; the others are bare and solitary. The two chief streets are broad, and much frequented, especially by horsemen; for every

Chilian is born a horseman, and is usually mounted on a steed worthy of a good rider.

Valparaiso houses are European in style, with flat Italian roofs. Broad steps lead up into a lofty entrance-hall on the first floor, from which, through large glass doors, the visitor passes into the drawing-room and other apartments. The drawing-room is the pride not only of every European settler, but of every native Chilian. The foot sinks into heavy and costly carpets; the walls are emblazoned with rich tapestry; the furniture and mirrors are of European make, and sumptuous in the extreme; and every table presents the evidence of refined taste in gorgeous albums, adorned with the choicest engravings.

As to the lower classes of the population, if we would obtain an idea of their manners and customs, we must stroll on a fête-day into one of their eating-houses.

In one corner, on the ground, crackles a tremendous fire, surrounded by innumerable pots and pans, between which are wooden spits with beef and pork, simmering and roasting with appetizing savour. A rude wooden frame-work, with a long broad plank on it, occupies the middle of the room, and is covered with a cloth, the original colour of which it is impossible to determine. This is the guest-table. The dinner is served up in the most primitive fashion imaginable, all the viands being heaped up in one dish; beans and rice, potatoes and roast beef, onions and paradise apples, forming a curious medley. The appetites of the guests are keen, and no time is wasted in talking. At the end of the repast, a goblet of wine or water passes from hand to hand; after which every tongue is loosened. In the evening a guitar strikes up, and dancing becomes general.

A singular custom prevails among the Chilians on the death of a little child. This incident, in most European families, is attended by much sorrow: the Chilian parents make it the occasion of a great festival. The deceased *angelito*, or little angel, is adorned in various ways. Its eyes, instead of being closed, are opened as wide as possible; its cheeks are painted red; then the cold rigid corpse is dressed in the finest clothes, crowned with flowers, and set up in a little chair in a flower-garlanded niche. The relatives and neighbours flock in, to wish the parents joy on the possession of such an angel; and, during the first night, they all indulge in the most extravagant dances, and feast with sounds of wildest merriment before the *angelito*.

Madame Pfeiffer heard from a merchant the following story:—A grave-digger, on his way to the churchyard with one of these deceased angelitos, tarried at a tavern to refresh himself with a cup of wine. The landlord inquired what he was carrying under his cloak, and on learning that it was an angelito, offered him a shilling for it. A bargain was soon struck; the landlord quickly fitted up a flowery niche in the drinking-saloon, and then took care that his neighbours should know what a treasure he had acquired. They came; they admired the angelito; they drank copiously in its honour. But the parents hearing of the affair, interfered, carried away their dead child, and summoned the landlord before the magistrate. The latter gravely heard the pleadings on both sides, and as no such case was mentioned in the statute-book, arranged it amicably, to the satisfaction of both parties.

SCENE IN TAHITI.

* * * * *

Wearying of Valparaiso, our restless and adventurous traveller, who was bent upon accomplishing a voyage round the world, took her passage for China in the Dutch barque *Lootpurt*, Captain Van Wyk Jurianse.

They sailed from Valparaiso on the 18th of March, and on the 26th of April came in sight of that gem of the South Seas, Tahiti, the Otaheite of Captain Cook, and the largest and most beautiful of the Society group. From the days of Bougainville, its discoverer, down to those of "the Earl and the Doctor," who recently published a narrative of their visit, it has been the theme of admiration for the charms of its scenery. It lifts its lofty summit out of a wealth of luxuriant vegetation, which descends to the very margin of a sea as blue as the sky above it. Cool green valleys penetrate into its mountain-recesses, and their slopes are loaded with groves of bread-fruit and cocoa-nut trees. The inhabitants, physically speaking, are not unworthy of their island-Eden; they are a tall, robust, and well-knit race, and would be comely but for their custom of flattening the nose as soon as the child is born. They have fine dark eyes, and thick jet-black hair. The colour of their skin is a copper-brown. Both sexes are tattooed, generally from the hips half down the legs, and frequently over the hands, feet, and other parts of the body; the devices being often very fanciful in design, and always artistically executed.

The women of Tahiti have always been notorious for their immodesty, and the island, notwithstanding the labours of zealous missionaries, continues to be the Polynesian Paphos. The French protectorate from which it suffers has not raised the moral standard of the population.

Madame Pfeiffer undertook an excursion to the Lake Vaihiria, assuming for the nonce a semi-masculine attire, which any less strong-minded and adventurous woman would probably have refused. She wore, she tells us, strong men's shoes, trousers, and a blouse, which was fastened high up about the hips. Thus equipped, she started off with her guide, crossing about two-and-thirty brooks before they entered the ravines leading into the interior of the island.

She noticed that as they advanced the fruit-trees disappeared, and instead, the slopes were covered with plantains, taros, and marantas; the last attaining a height of twelve feet, and growing so luxuriantly that it is with some difficulty the traveller makes his way through the tangle. The taro, which is carefully cultivated, averages two or three feet high, and has fine large leaves and tubers like those of the potato, but not so good when roasted. There is much gracefulness in the appearance of the plantain, or banana, which varies from twelve to fifteen feet in height, and has leaves like those of the palm, but a brittle reed-like stem, about eight inches in diameter. It attains its full growth in the first year, bears fruit in the second, and then dies. Thus its life is as brief as it is useful.

Through one bright mountain-stream, which swept along the ravine over a stony bed, breaking up into eddies and tiny whirlpools, and in some places attaining a depth of three feet, Madame Pfeiffer and her guide waded or half-swam two-and-sixty times. The resolute spirit of the woman, however, never failed her; and though the path at every step became more difficult and dangerous, she persisted in pressing forward. She clambered over rocks and stones; she forced her way through inter-tangled bushes; and though severely wounded in her hands and feet, never hesitated for a moment. In two places the ravine narrowed so considerably that the entire space was filled by the brawling torrent. It was here that the islanders, during their struggle against French occupation, threw up stone walls five feet in height, as a barrier against the enemy.

In eight hours the bold traveller and her guide had walked, waded, and clambered fully eighteen miles, and had attained an elevation of eighteen hundred feet. The lake itself was not visible until they stood upon its shores, as it lies bosomed in a deep hollow, among lofty and precipitous mountains which descend with startling abruptness to the very brink of its dark, deep waters. To cross the lake it is necessary to put one's trust in one's swimming powers, or in a curiously frail kind of boat, which the natives prepare with equal rapidity and skill. Madame Pfeiffer, however, was nothing if not adventurous. Whatever there was to be dared, she immediately dared. At her request, the guide made the usual essay at boat-building. He tore off some plantain branches, bound them together with long tough grass, laid a few leaves upon them, launched them in the water, and requested Madame Pfeiffer to embark. She confesses to having felt a little hesitation, but without saying a word, she stepped on board. Then her guide took to the water like a duck, and pushed her forward. The passage across the lake, and back again, was in this way accomplished without any accident.

Having satiated herself with admiring the lake and its surrounding scenery, she retired to a little nook roofed over with leaves, where her guide quickly kindled a good fire in the usual Indian fashion. He cut a small piece of wood to a fine point, and then selecting a second piece, grooved it with a narrow and not very deep furrow. In this he rubbed the pointed stick until the fragments detached during the process began to smoke. These he flung into a heap of dry leaves and grass previously collected, and swung the whole several times round in the air, until it broke out into flames. The entire process did not occupy above two minutes. Gathering a few plantains, these were roasted for supper; after which Madame Pfeiffer withdrew to her solitary couch of dry leaves, to sleep as best she might. It is impossible not to wonder at the marvellous physical capability of this adventurous woman, no less than at her courage, her resolution, and her perseverance. How many of her sex could bear for a week the fatigue and exposure to which she subjected herself year after year?

The next morning she accomplished the return journey in safety.

* * * * *

HONG-KONG

On the 17th of May she left Tahiti, the Dutch vessel in which she had embarked being bound via the Philippines. They passed this rich and radiant group of islands on the 1st of July, and the next day entered the dangerous China Sea. A few days afterwards they reached Hong-Kong, which has been an English settlement since 1842. Here Madame Pfeiffer made no long stay, for she desired to see China and the Chinese with as little intermixture of the European element as possible. So she ascended the Pearl river, the banks of which are covered with immense plantations of rice, and studded with quaint little country-houses, of the genuine Chinese pattern, with sloping, pointed roofs, and mosaics of variously coloured tiles, to Canton, one of the great commercial centres of the Flowery Land. As she approached she surveyed with wonder the animated scene before her. The river was crowded with ships and inhabited boats. Junks there were, almost as large as the old Spanish galleons, with poops impending far over the water, and covered in with a roof, like a house. Men-of-war there were, flat, broad, and long, mounted with twenty or thirty guns, and adorned in the usual Chinese fashion, with two large painted eyes at the prow, that they may be the better able to find their way. Mandarins' boats she saw, with doors, and sides, and windows gaily painted, with carved galleries, and tiny silken flags fluttering from every point. And flower-boats she also saw; their upper galleries decked with flowers, garlands, and arabesques, as if these were barks fitted out for the service of Titania and her fairy company. The interior is divided into one large apartment and a few cabinets, which are lighted by windows of fantastic design. Mirrors and silk hangings embellish the walls, while the enchanting scene is completed with an ample garniture of glass chandeliers and coloured paper lanterns, interspersed with lovely little baskets of fresh flowers.

It is not necessary to attempt a description of Canton, with its pagodas, houses, shops, and European factories. Let us direct our attention to the manners, customs, and peculiarities of its inhabitants. As to dress and appearance, the costume of both sexes, among the lower orders, consists of full trousers and long upper garments, and is chiefly remarkable for its "excessive filth." Baths and ablutions have no charm for the Chinaman; he scorns to wear a shirt, and he holds by his trousers until they drop from his body. The men's upper garments reach a little below the knee, the women's about half way down the calf. They are made of nankeen, or dark blue, brown, or black silk. During the cold season both men and women wear one summer garment over the other, keeping the whole together with a girdle; in the extreme heat, however, they suffer them to float as free as "Nora Creina's robes" in Moore's pretty ballad.

The men keep their heads shaved, with the exception of a small patch at the back, where the hair is carefully cultivated and plaited into a cue. The thicker and longer this cue is, the prouder is its owner; false hair and black ribbon, therefore, are all deftly worked into it, with the result of forming an appendage which often reaches down to the ankles! While at work the owner twists it round his neck, but on entering a room he lets it down again, as it would be contrary to all the laws of etiquette and courtesy for a person to make his appearance with his cue twisted up. The women comb their hair entirely back from their forehead, and fasten it to the head in the most artistic plaits. The process occupies a considerable time, but when the hair is once dressed it is not retouched for a whole week. Both men and women frequently go about with heads uncovered; but sometimes they wear hats of thin bamboo, three feet in diameter. These are not only an adequate protection against sun and rain, but are exceedingly durable.

Large numbers of Chinese live a kind of aquatic life, and make their home on board a river-boat. The husband goes on shore to his work, and his wife meantime adds to the income of the family by ferrying persons from bank to bank, or letting out the boat to pleasure parties—always reserving one half of its accommodation for herself and household. Room is not very abundant, as the whole boat does not exceed twenty-five feet in length; but everywhere the greatest order and cleanliness are apparent, each separate plank being enthusiastically scrubbed and washed every morning. It is worth notice how each inch of space is turned to the best advantage, room being made even for the *lares* and *penates*. All the washing and cooking are done during the day; yet the pleasure party is never in the least degree inconvenienced.

Of course our traveller was attracted by the diminutiveness of the feet of the Chinese women, and she had an opportunity of examining one of these tiny monstrosities *in naturâ*. Four of the toes were bent under the sole of the foot, to which they were firmly pressed, and simultaneously with which they appeared to have grown, if growth it can be called; the great toe alone remained in its natural state. The fore part of the foot had been so swathed and compressed by tight bandages, that, instead of expanding in length and breadth, it had shot upwards, so as to form a large lump at the instep, where it became, so to speak, a portion of the leg; the lower part of the foot was scarcely five inches long, and an inch and a half broad. The feet are always encased in white linen or silk, with silk bandages over all, and are then stuffed into pretty little shoes with very high heels. "To my astonishment," says Madame Pfeiffer, "these deformed beings tripped about, as if in defiance of us broad-footed creatures, with tolerable ease, the only difference in their gait being that they waddled like geese; they even ran up and down stairs without a stick." She adds, that the value of a bride is reckoned by the smallness of her feet.

It was characteristic of Madame Pfeiffer that she found means to see much which no European woman had ever seen before. She obtained access even to a Buddhist temple,—that of Houan, reputed to be one of the finest in China. The sacred enclosure is surrounded by a high wall. The visitor enters first a large outer court, at the extremity of which a huge gateway opens upon an inner court. Beneath the arch stand two statues of war-gods, each eighteen feet high, with terribly distorted faces and the most menacing attitudes; these are supposed to prevent the approach of evil genii. A second portal, of similar construction, under which are placed the "four heavenly kings," leads to a third court, surrounding the principal temple, a structure one hundred feet in length, and of equal breadth. On rows of wooden pillars is supported a flat roof, from which glass lamps, lustres, artificial flowers, and brightly-coloured ribbons hang suspended. All about the area are scattered statues, altars, vases of flowers, censers, candelabra, and other accessories.

But the eye is chiefly attracted by the three altars in the foreground, with the three coloured statues behind them, of Buddha, seated, as emblematic of Past, Present, and Future. On the occasion of Madame Pfeiffer's visit a service was being performed,—a funeral ceremony in honour of a mandarin's deceased wife, and at his expense. Before the altars on the right and left stood several priests, in garments strangely resembling, as did the ceremonial observances, those of the Roman Church. The mandarin himself, attended by two servants armed with large fans, prayed before the central altar. He kissed the ground repeatedly, and each time he did so three sweet-scented wax-tapers were put into his hand. After raising them in the air, he handed them to the priests, who then stationed them, unlighted, before the Buddha images. Meantime, the temple resounded with the blended strains of three musicians, one of whom struck a metal ball, the other scraped a stringed instrument, and the third educed shrill notes from a kind of flute.

This principal temple is surrounded by numerous smaller sanctuaries, each decorated with images of deities, rudely wrought, but glowing with gilt and vivid colours. Special reverence seems to be accorded to Kwanfootse, a demigod of War, and the four-and-twenty gods of Mercy. These latter have four, six, and even eight arms. In the Temple of Mercy Madame Pfeiffer met with an unpleasant adventure. A Bonze had offered her and her companions a couple of wax tapers to light in honour of the god. They were on the point of complying, as a matter of civility, when an American missionary, who made one of the party, snatched them roughly from their hands, and gave them back to the priests, protesting that such compliance was idolatrous. The Bonze, in high indignation, closed the door, and summoned his brethren, who hurried in from all sides, and jostled and pushed and pressed, while using the most violent language. It was not without difficulty they forced their way through the crowd, and escaped from the temple.

The guide next led the curiosity-hunters to the so-called House of the Sacred Swine. The greatest attention is paid to these porcine treasures, and they reside in a spacious stone hall; but not the less is the atmosphere heavy with odours that are not exactly those of Araby the Blest. Throughout their sluggish existence the swine are carefully fed and cherished, and no cruel knife cuts short the thread of their destiny. At the time of Madame Pfeiffer's visit only one pair were enjoying their *otium cum dignitate*, and the number rarely exceeds three pairs.

Peeping into the interior of a Bonze's house, the company came upon an opium-smoker. He lay stretched upon a mat, with small tea-cups beside him, some fruit, a tiny lamp, and several miniature-headed pipes, from one of which he was inhaling the intoxicating smoke. It is said that some of the Chinese opium-smokers consume as much as twenty or thirty grains daily. This poor wretch was not wholly unconscious of the presence of visitors; and, laying by his pipe, he raised himself from the ground, and dragged his body to a chair. With deadly pale face and fixed, staring eyes, he presented a miserable appearance.

* * * * *

Our traveller also visited a pagoda,—the Half-Way Pagoda; so called by the English because it is situated half-way between Canton and Whampoa. On a small hillock, in the midst of vast tracts of rice, it raises its nine stories to a height of one hundred and seventy feet. Though formerly of great repute, it is now deserted. The interior has been stripped of statues and ornaments, and the floors having been removed, the visitor sees to the very summit. Externally, each stage is indicated by a small balcony without railing, access being obtained by steep and narrow flights of stairs. A picturesque effect is produced by these projections, as everybody knows who has examined a "willow-pattern" plate. They are built of coloured bricks, which are laid in rows, with their points jutting obliquely outwards, and faced with variegated tiles.

Even more interesting was Madame Pfeiffer's peep into the "domestic interior" of Mandarin Howqua.

The house was of large size, but only one story high, with wide and splendid terraces. The windows looked into the inner courts. At the entrance were two painted images of gods to ward off evil spirits, like the horse-shoe formerly suspended to the cottages and barns of our English peasants.

The front part was divided into several reception rooms, without front walls; and adjoining these, bloomed bright and gaily-ordered parterres of flowers and shrubs. The magnificent terraces above also bloomed with blossom, and commanded a lively view of the crowded river, and of the fine scenery that spreads around Canton. Elegant little cabinets surrounded these rooms, being separated by thin partitions, through which the eye could easily penetrate, and frequently embellished with gay and skilfully-executed paintings. The material used was chiefly bamboo, which was as delicate as gauze, and copiously decorated with painted flowers or beautifully-written proverbs.

The chairs and sofas were numerous, and of really artistic workmanship. Some of the arm-chairs were cunningly wrought out of a single piece of wood. The seats of others were beautiful marble slabs; of others, again, fine coloured tiles or porcelain. Articles of European manufacture, such as handsome mirrors, clocks, vases, and tables of Florentine mosaic or variegated marble, were plentiful. There was also a remarkable collection of lamps and lanterns pendent from the ceilings, consisting—these lamps and lanterns—of glass, transparent horn, and coloured gauze or paper, ornamented with glass beads, fringe, and tassels. And as the walls were also largely supplied with lamps, the apartments, when lighted up, assumed a truly fairy-like character.

CHINESE HOUSE AND GARDEN

The mandarin's pleasure-garden stretched along the river-side. Its cultivation was perfect, but no taste was shown in its arrangement. Wherever the visitor turned, kiosks, summer-houses, and bridges confronted her. Every path and open spot were lined with large and small flower-pots, in which grew flowers and liliputian fruit-trees of all kinds. In the art of dwarfing trees, if such distortion and crippling of Nature deserves to be called an art, the Chinese are certainly most accomplished experts; but what can we think of the taste, or want of taste, which prefers pigmies three feet high to the lofty and far-shadowing trees which embellish our English parks and gardens? Why should a civilized people put Nature in fetters, and delight in checking her growth, in limiting her spontaneous energies?

Here are some particulars about the tea-plant:—In the plantations around Canton, it is not allowed to grow higher than six feet, and is consequently cut at intervals. Its leaves are considered good from the third to the eighth year; and the plant is then cut down, in order that it may throw off new shoots, or else it is rooted out. Three gatherings take place in the year; the first in March, the second in April, and the third, which lasts for three months, in May. So fine and delicate are the leaves of the first gathering, that they might easily be mistaken for the blossom; which undoubtedly has originated the error that the so-called "bloom or imperial tea" consists of the flowers and not of the leaves of the plant.

When gathered, the leaves are thrown for a few seconds into boiling water, and then placed on flat iron plates, inserted slantwise in stone-work. While roasting over a gentle fire, they are continually stirred. As soon as they begin to curl a little, they are scattered over large planks, and each single leaf is rolled together; a process so rapidly accomplished that it requires a person's sole attention to detect that only one leaf is rolled up at a time. This completed, all the leaves are again placed in the pans. Black tea takes some time to roast; and the green is frequently coloured with Prussian blue, an exceedingly small quantity of which is added during the second roasting. Last of all, the tea is once more shaken out upon the boards, and submitted to a careful inspection, the leaves that are not entirely closed being rolled over again.

SINGAPORE

Madame Pfeiffer had an opportunity of tasting a cup of tea made after the most approved Chinese fashion. A small quantity was dropped into a delicate porcelain cup, boiling water was poured upon it, and a tightly-fitting cover then adjusted to the cup. After a few seconds, the infusion was ready for drinking—neither milk, cream, nor sugar being added.

* * * * *

But we must tarry no longer within the borders of the Celestial Empire. We have to follow Madame Pfeiffer in her wanderings over many seas and through many countries,—for in the course of her adventurous career she saw more of "men and cities" than even the much-travelling Ulysses,—and our limits confine us to brief notices of the most remarkable places she visited.

From China she sailed for the East Indies.

On her way she "looked in" at Singapore, a British settlement, where gather the traders of many Asiatic nations. The scenery which stretches around it is of a rich and agreeable character, and the island on which it is situated excels in fertility of vegetation. A saunter among the plantations of cloves and nutmegs is very pleasant, the air breathing a peculiar balsamic fragrance. The nutmeg-tree is about the size of a good apricot-bush, and from top to bottom is a mass of foliage; the branches grow very low down the stem, and the leaves glitter as if they were varnished. The fruit closely resembles an apricot, covered with spots of yellowish-brown. It bursts on attaining maturity, and then reveals a round kernel, of the size of a nut, embedded in a network, sold as mace, of a beautiful red colour. This network of fibrous material is carefully separated from the nutmeg, and dried in the shade,—being frequently sprinkled with sea-water, to prevent the colour deepening into black, instead of changing into yellow. The nutmeg is likewise dried, exposed a while to the action of smoke, and dipped several times into sea-water containing a weak solution of lime, to prevent it from turning mouldy.

The clove-tree is smaller, and less copiously provided with foliage, than the nutmeg-tree. The buds form what are known to us as cloves; and, of course, are gathered before they have had time to blossom. The areca-nut palm is also plentiful in Singapore. It grows in clusters of from ten to twenty nuts; is somewhat larger than a nutmeg, and of a bright colour, almost resembling gilt.

The Chinese and the natives of the Eastern Islands chew it with betel-leaf and calcined mussel-shells. With a small quantity of the latter they strew the leaf; a very small piece of the nut is added, and the whole is made into a little packet, which they put into their mouth.

Madame Pfeiffer also inspected a sago manufactory. The unprepared farina, which is the pith of the sago palm, is imported from a neighbouring island. The tree is cut down when it is seven years old, split from top to bottom, and the pith extracted from it. Then it is freed from the fibres, pressed in large frames, and dried at the fire or in the sun. At Singapore this pith or meal, which is of a yellowish tint, is steeped in water for several days until completely blanched; it is then once more dried by the fire or in the sun, passed under a large wooden roller, and through a hair sieve. When it has become white and fine, it is placed in a kind of linen winnowing-fan, which is kept damp in a peculiar manner. The workman takes a mouthful of water, and "spirts it out like fine rain over the fan;" the meal being alternately shaken and moistened until it assumes the character of small globules. These are stirred round in large flat pans, until they are dried. Then they are passed through a second sieve, not quite so fine as the first, and the larger globules are separated from the rest.

Pepper and gambir plantations are also among the "sights" of Singapore. The pepper-tree is a small bush-like plant, which, when carefully trained, springs to a height of eighteen feet. The pepper-pods grow in small clusters, and change from red to green, and then to black. White pepper is nothing more than the black pepper blanched by frequent steeping in sea-water. The gambir does not grow taller than eight feet. The leaves, which are used in dyeing, are first stripped from the stalk, and then boiled down in large coppers. The thick juice is placed in white wooden vessels, and dried in the sun; then it is divided into slips about three inches long, and packed up.

Singapore is an island of *fruits*. It boasts of the delicious mangosteen, which almost melts in the mouth, and delights the palate with its exquisite flavour. It boasts, too, of splendid pine-apples, frequently weighing as much as four pounds. Also of sauersop, as big as the biggest pine-apples, green outside, and white or pale yellow inside, with a taste and fragrance like that of strawberries. Nor must the gumaloh be forgotten: it is divided, like the orange, into sections, but is five times as large, and not quite so sweet. Finally, we must refer to the custard-apple, which is very white (though full of black pips), very soft, and very enticing in flavour.

* * * * *

From Singapore we follow Madame Pfeiffer to Point de Galle, in Ceylon. The appearance of this fair and fertile island from the sea is the theme of every traveller's praise. "It was one of the most magnificent sights I ever beheld," says Madame Pfeiffer, "to see the island soaring gradually from the sea, with its mountain-ranges growing more and more distinctly defined, their summits lighted by the sun, while the dense cocoa-groves, and hills and plains, lay shrouded in shadow." Above the whole towers the purple mass of Adam's Peak; and the eye rests in every direction on the most luxuriant foliage, with verdurous glades, and slopes carpeted with flowers.

Point de Galle presents a curious mixture of races. Cingalese, Kanditons, Tamils from South India, and Moormen, with crimson caftans and shaven crowns, form the bulk of the crowds that throng its streets; but, besides these, there are Portuguese, Chinese, Jews, Arabs, Parsees, Englishmen, Malays, Dutchmen, and half-caste burghers, and now and then a veiled Arabian woman, or a Veddah, one of the aboriginal inhabitants of the island. Sir Charles Dilke speaks of "silent crowds of tall and graceful girls, wearing, as we at first supposed, white petticoats and bodices; their hair carried off the face with a decorated hoop, and caught at the back by a high tortoise-shell comb. As they drew near, moustaches began to show, and I saw that they were men; whilst walking with them were women naked to the waist, combless, and far more rough and 'manly' than their husbands. Petticoat and chignon are male institutions in Ceylon."

* * * * *

Madame Pfeiffer, with unresting energy, visited Colombo and Kandy, the chief towns of the island. At the latter she obtained admission to the Temple of Dagoba, which contains a precious relic of the god Buddha—namely, one of his teeth. The sanctuary containing this sacred treasure is a small chamber or cell, less than twenty feet in breadth. It is enveloped in darkness, as there are no windows; and the door is curtained inside, for the more effectual exclusion of the light. Rich tapestry covers the walls and ceiling. But the chief object is the altar, which glitters with plates of silver, and is incrusted about the edges with precious stones. Upon it stands a bell-shaped case about three feet in height, and three feet in diameter at the base. It is made of silver, elaborately gilt, and decorated with a number of costly jewels. A peacock in the middle blazes with jewels. Six smaller cases, reputed to be of gold, are enclosed within the large one, and under the last is the tooth of Buddha. As it is as large as that of a great bull, one trembles to think how monstrous must have been the jaw of the Indian creed-founder!

NATIVE BOAT. MADRAS.

* * * * *

Madame Ida Pfeiffer arrived at Madras on the 30th of October. She describes the process of disembarkation; but as her details are few, and refer to a comparatively distant date, we propose to rely on the narrative of a recent traveller.

From time immemorial, he says, the system of landing and embarking passengers and cargo has been by means of native Massulah boats, constructed of mango wood, calked with straw, and sewn together with cocoa-nut fibre. The ships drop their anchors in the roads half a mile from the shore; the Massulah boat pulls off alongside, receives its cargo at the gangway, and is then beached through the surf. It is no uncommon circumstance for the boat alongside, assisted by the rolling of the ship, to rise and fall twenty-five feet relatively to the height of the ship's deck at each undulation. Ladies are lashed into chairs, and from the ship's yard-arm lowered into the boat. In 1860 some improvement was effected by the construction of an iron pier, about nine hundred feet in length, and twenty feet in height. But a spacious and sheltered harbour is now being provided, by means of piers running out from the shore five hundred yards north and south respectively of the screw pile pier now existing, so as to enclose a rectangular area of one thousand yards in length by eight hundred and thirty yards in width, or one hundred and seventy acres. The foundation-stone was laid by the Prince of Wales in the course of his Indian progress in 1876.

Madame Pfeiffer stayed but a few hours at Madras, and her notes respecting it are of no value. We will proceed at once to Calcutta, the "City of Palaces," as it has been called, and the capital of our Indian Empire.

She speaks of the Viceroy's Palace as a magnificent building, and one that would ornament any city in the world. Other noticeable edifices are the Town Hall, the Hospital, the Museum, Ochterlony's Monument, the Mint, and the Cathedral. Ochterlony's Monument is a plain stone column, one hundred and sixty-five feet high, erected in commemoration of a sagacious statesman and an able soldier. From its summit, to which access is obtained by two hundred and twenty-two steps, may be obtained a noble view of the city, the broad reaches of the Ganges, and the fertile plains of Bengal.

The Cathedral is an imposing pile. Its architecture is Gothic, and the interior produces a very fine effect by the harmony of its proportions and the richness of its details. The ill-famed "Black Hole," in which the Rajah Surajah Dowlah confined one hundred and fifty English men and women, when he obtained possession of Calcutta in 1756—confining them in a narrow and noisome cell, which poisoned them with its malarious atmosphere, so that by morning only a few remained alive—is now part of a warehouse. But an obelisk stands at the entrance, inscribed with the names of the victims.

The fashionable promenade at Calcutta is the Maidan. It runs along the bank of the Hooghly, and is bounded on the other side by rows of palatial mansions. It commands a good view of the Viceroy's Palace, the Cathedral, the Ochterlony Column, the strong defensive works of Fort William; and is altogether a very interesting and attractive spot.

Every evening, before sunset, thither wends the fashionable world of Calcutta. The impassive European, with all the proud consciousness of a conquering race; the half-Europeanized baboo; the deposed rajah,—all may be seen driving to and fro in splendid equipages, drawn by handsome steeds, and followed by servants in gay Oriental attire. The rajahs and "nabobs" are usually dressed in gold-embroidered robes of silk, over which are thrown the costliest Indian shawls. Ladies and gentlemen, on English horses of the best blood, canter along the road, or its turfen borders; while crowds of dusky natives gather in all directions, or leisurely move homewards after their day's work. A bright feature of the scene is the animated appearance of the Hooghly: first-class East Indiamen are lying at anchor, ships are arriving or preparing for departure, the native craft incessantly ply to and fro, and a Babel of voices of different nationalities rises on the air.

Here is a picture of the Maidan, drawn by another lady-traveller, Mrs. Murray Mitchell:—

THE MAIDAN, CALCUTTA

It is, she says, a noble expanse, which, about a hundred years ago, was a wild swampy jungle, famous only for snipe-shooting. Strange to say, it is not, like most Indian plains, burned up and brown, but, from its vicinity to the river, and the frequent showers that visit it, as fresh and green as an English park. It has a few fine tanks, and is sprinkled with some leafy trees; these, however, not so numerous as they were before the cyclones of 1864 and 1867, which swept away its chief natural beauties. Several broad well-kept drives intersect it, and it is ornamented by some graceful gardens and a few handsome columns and statues. Indeed, the Maidan is the centre of all that is grand and imposing; the shabby and the unsightly is kept behind, out of view. Facing it, along its eastern marge, stand the noble pillared palaces of Chowringhee. At one end stands the handsome new Court House; also the Town Hall, and other buildings of less pretence; and, further on, the noble pile of Government House, with four handsome entrance gates, and surrounded by shrubberies and gardens. In front spread the Eden Gardens, a delightful addition to the beauties both of Government House and the Esplanade. From this point the business part of Calcutta extends in a northerly direction, including Dalhousie Square, with its many buildings, among which conspicuous stands the domed Post Office—the vista closing gracefully with the shapely spire of St. Andrew's Church. At the further extremity, nearly two miles across the verdant expanse, are seen the Cathedral, with its noble spire, the General Hospital, and the Jail; and still further, the richly-wooded suburbs of Kidderpore and Alipore. Fort William fronts toward the river, and with its ramparts and buildings forms a striking object; while the whole is bordered and "beautified" by the broad river, with its crowd of masts and flags, its almost innumerable boats, its landing-ghats, and all its life and motion.

* * * * *

BENARES

From Calcutta, Madame Pfeiffer proceeded to the city of temples, the sacred city of Hinduism—Benares. She visited several temples, but found them all agreeing in their leading details. That of Vishnu has two towers connected by colonnades, the summits of which are covered with gold plates. Inside are several images of Vishnu and Siva, wreathed with flowers, and strewn over with grains of rice and wheat. Images in metal or stone of the sacred bull are plentiful everywhere; and living bulls wander about freely, the object of special care and adoration. They are free to stray where they will, not in the temple precincts only, but also in the streets.

Among the other buildings, the one most worthy of notice is the Mosque of Aurengzebe, famous on account of its two minarets, which are 150 feet in height, and reported to be the slenderest in the world. They resemble a couple of needles, and certainly better deserve the name than that of Cleopatra at Alexandria. Narrow winding staircases in the interior lead to the summit, on which a small platform, with a balustrade about a foot high, is erected. From this vantage-point a noble view of the city, it is said, may be obtained; but few persons, we should think, have heads cool enough to enjoy it. With all Madame Pfeiffer's adventurousness, she did not essay this perilous experiment.

The Observatory, constructed for the great Mohammedan emperor Akbar, is also an object of interest. It is not furnished, like a European observatory, with the usual astronomical instruments, telescopes, rain-gauges, anemometers, and the like, the handiwork of cunning artificers in glass and metal; but everything is of stone—solid, durable stone. On a raised terrace stand circular tables, semicircular and quadratic curves, all of stone, and all inscribed with mystic signs and characters.

Benares is celebrated for its bazaars, in which are exhibited some of the rarest productions of the East; but its principal attraction is its sanctity, and crowds of pilgrims resort to its temples, and cleanse themselves of their sins by bathing in the fast-flowing Ganges. To die at Benares is regarded as a passport to heaven; and one of the most frequent sights is the burning of a corpse on the river-bank, with ceremonies proportioned to the rank and wealth of the deceased—the ashes being afterwards committed to the holy waters. Benares is also famous for its palaces. Of these the most splendid is that which the rajah inhabits. It was visited by Madame Pfeiffer, who appears to have gone everywhere and seen everybody at her own sweet will and pleasure, and she was even admitted to the rajah's presence.

A handsomely-decorated boat, she says, awaited her and her fellow-traveller at the bank of the river. They crossed; a palanquin was ready to receive them. Soon they arrived at the stately gateway which forms the entrance to the palace. The interior proved to be a labyrinth of irregular courts and small unsymmetrical chambers. In one of the courts a hall, surrounded by plain columns, served as a reception-room. This was cumbrously loaded with lamps, glass lustres, and European furniture; on the walls hung some wretched pictures, framed and glazed. Presently the rajah made his appearance, accompanied by his brother, and attended by a long train of courtiers. The two princes were gorgeously attired; they wore wide trousers, long under and short over garments, all of satin, covered with gold embroidery. The rajah himself, aged thirty-five, wore short silken cuffs, glowing with gold, and trimmed with diamonds; several large brilliants shone on his fingers, and rich gold embroidery was woven about his shoes. His brother, a youth of nineteen, wore a white turban, with a costly clasp of diamonds and pearls. Large pearls hung from his ears; rich massive bracelets clasped his wrists.

The guests having taken their seats, a large silver basin was brought in, with elaborately-wrought narghillies, and they were invited to smoke. This honour they declined. The rajah then smoked in solitary dignity—his pipe being changed as soon as he had taken a few whiffs.

A nautchni, or dance by nautches, was next provided for the visitors' entertainment. There were three musicians and two dancers. The latter were dressed in gay gold-woven muslin robes, with wide silk gold-broidered trousers, reaching to the ground, and quite covering their bare feet. One of the musicians beat a couple of small drums; the others played on four-stringed instruments not unlike a violin. They stood close behind the dancers, and their music was wholly innocent of melody or harmony; but to the rhythm, which was strongly accentuated, the dancers moved their arms, hands, and fingers in a very animated manner, and at intervals their feet, so as to ring the numerous tiny bells that cover them. Their attitudes were not ungraceful. The performance lasted a quarter of an hour, after which they accompanied the dance with what was intended for singing, but sounded like shrieking. Meantime, sweetmeats, fruits, and sherbet were handed round.

As a contrast to this gay scene, Madame Pfeiffer describes the performance of the wretched fanatics called fakeers. These men inflict upon themselves the most extraordinary tortures. Thus: they stick an iron hook through their flesh, and allow themselves to be suspended by it at a height of twenty or five-and-twenty feet. {105} Or for long hours they stand upon one foot in the burning sunshine, with their arms rigidly extended in the air. Or they hold heavy weights in various positions, swing round and round for hours together, and tear the flesh from their bodies with red-hot pincers. Madame Pfeiffer saw two of these unfortunate victims of a diseased imagination. One held a heavy axe over his head, in the attitude of a workman bent on felling a tree; in this position he stood, rigid as a statue. The other held the point of his toe to his nose.

* * * * *

In her tour through India our traveller passed through Allahabad, situated at the junction of the Jumna and the Ganges, and the resort of many pilgrims; Agra, where she admired, as so many travellers have admired, the lovely Taj-Mahal, erected by the Sultan Jehan in memory of his favourite wife,—and the Pearl Mosque, with its exquisitely delicate carving; Delhi, the ancient capital of the Moguls, which figured so conspicuously in the history of the Sepoy rebellion; the cave-temples of Ajunta and Ellora; and the great commercial emporium of Bombay.

Quitting the confines of British India, Madame Pfeiffer, ever in quest of the new and strange, sailed to Bassora, and ascended the historic Tigris, so named from the swiftness of its course, to Bagdad, that quaint, remote Oriental city, which is associated with so many wonderful legends and not less wonderful "travellers' tales." This was of old the residence of the great caliph, Haroun-al-Raschid, a ruler of no ordinary sagacity, and the hero of many a tradition, whom "The Thousand and One Nights" have made familiar to every English boy. It is still a populous and wealthy city; many of its houses are surrounded by blooming gardens; its shops are gay with the products of the Eastern loom; and it descends in terraces to the bank of the river, which flows in the shade of orchards and groves of palm. Over all extends the arch of a glowing sky.

From Bagdad an excursion to the ruins of Babylon is natural enough. They consist of massive fragments of walls and columns, strewn on either side of the Euphrates.

CAVE TEMPLE AT ELLORA

On the 17th of June our heroic traveller joined a caravan which was bound for Mosul, a distance of three hundred miles, occupying from twelve to fourteen days. The journey is one of much difficulty and no little danger, across a desert country of the most lifeless character. We shall relate a few of Madame Pfeiffer's experiences.

One day she repaired to a small village in search of food. After wandering from hut to hut, she obtained a small quantity of milk and three eggs. She laid the eggs in hot ashes, and covered them over; filled her leathern flask from the Tigris; and, thus loaded, returned to the encampment formed by the caravan. She ate her eggs and drank her milk with an appetite for which an epicure would be thankful.

The mode of making butter in vogue at this village was very peculiar. The cream was put into a leathern bottle, and shaken about on the ground until the butter consolidated. It was then put into another bottle filled with water, and finally turned out as white as snow.

Next day, when they rested during the heat, the guide of the caravan endeavoured to procure her a little shelter from the glare of the pitiless sun by laying a small cover over a couple of poles stuck into the ground. But the place shaded was so small, and the tent so frail, that she was compelled to sit quietly in one position, as the slightest movement would have involved it in ruin. Shortly afterwards, when she wished for some refreshment, nothing could be procured but lukewarm water, bread so hard that it could not be eaten until thoroughly soaked, and a cucumber without salt or vinegar.

At a village near Kerka the caravan tarried for two days. On the first day Madame Pfeiffer's patience was sorely tried. All the women of the place flocked to examine the stranger. First they inspected her clothes, then wanted to take the turban off her head; and, in fact, proved themselves most troublesome intruders. At last Madame Pfeiffer seized one of them by the arm, and turned her out of her tent so quickly that she had no time to think of resistance. By the eloquence of gesture our traveller made the others understand that, unless they withdrew at once, a similarly abrupt dismissal awaited them. She then drew a circle round her tent, and forbade them to cross it; an injunction which was strictly respected.

She had now only to settle with the wife of her guide, who had besieged her the whole day, pressing as near as possible, and petitioning for some of her "things." Fortunately her husband came on the scene, and to him Madame Pfeiffer preferred her complaint, threatening to leave his house and seek shelter elsewhere,—well knowing that the Arabs consider this a great disgrace. He immediately ordered his wife to desist, and the traveller was at peace. "I always succeeded," says Madame Pfeiffer, "in obtaining my own will. I found that energy and boldness influence all people, whether Arabs, Persians, Bedaween, or others." But for this strong will, this indomitable resolution, Madame Pfeiffer assuredly could not have succeeded in the enterprises she so daringly undertook. Even for a man to have accomplished them would have earned our praise; what shall we not say when they were conceived and carried out by a woman?

Towards evening, she says, to her great delight a caldron of mutton was set on the fire. For eight days she had eaten nothing but bread, cucumbers, and some dates; and therefore had a great desire for a hot and more nutritious meal. But her appetite was greatly diminished when she saw their style of cookery. The old woman (her guide's mother) threw several handfuls of small grain, and a large quantity of onions, into a panful of water to soften. In about half an hour she thrust her dirty hands into the water, and mixed the whole together, now and then taking a mouthful, and after chewing it, spitting it back again into the pan. Then she took a dirty rag, strained through it the delicate mixture, and poured it over the meat in the larger vessel. Madame Pfeiffer had firmly resolved not to touch the dish, but when it was ready her longing for food was so great, and so savoury was the smell, that she reflected that what she had already eaten was probably not a whit cleaner; in short, for once she proved false to her resolution. Eating, she was filled; and the viands gave her increased strength.

* * * * *

On the 28th of June the caravan reached Erbil, the ancient Arbela, where Alexander the Great defeated Darius and his Persian host. Next day they crossed a broad river, on rafts of inflated skins, fastened together with poles, and covered with reeds, canes, and plank. Rapidly traversing the shrubless, herbless plains of Mesopotamia, they reached at length the town of Mosul, the point from which travellers proceed to visit the ruins of Nineveh.

These have been so carefully explored and ably described by Layard and the late George Smith, that it is needless to quote Madame Ida Pfeiffer's superficial observations at any length. According to Strabo, Nineveh was the greatest city in the Old World—larger even than Babylon; the circumference of its walls was a three days' journey, and those walls were defended by fifteen hundred towers. Now all is covered with earth, and the ranges of hills and mounds that stretch across the wide gray plain on the bank of the Tigris do but cover the ruins of the vast Assyrian capital. Mr. Layard began his excavations in 1846, and his labourers, digging deep into the hills, soon opened up spacious and stately apartments, the marble walls of which were embellished from top to bottom with sculptures, revealing a complete panorama of Assyrian life! Kings with their crowns and sceptres, gods swooping on broad pinions, warriors equipped with their arms and shields, were there; also stirring representations of battles and hunting expeditions, of the storming of fortresses, of triumphal processions; though, unfortunately for artistic effect, neither proportion, perspective, nor correct drawing had been observed. The hills are scarcely three times higher than the men; the fields reach to the clouds; the trees are no taller than the lotus-flowers; and the heads of men and animals are all alike, and all in profile. Intermingled with these scenes of ancient civilization are inscriptions of great interest, in the cuneiform or wedge-shaped character.

* * * * *

A caravan starting from Mosul for Tabreez, Madame Ida Pfeiffer determined on joining it, though warned that it would traverse a country containing not a single European. But, as we have already had abundant evidence, Madame Pfeiffer knew not what fear was. Nothing could daunt her fixed purpose. She had made up her mind to go to Persia; and to Persia she would go. She started with the caravan on the 8th of July, and next day crossed the hills that intervene between Mesopotamia and Kurdistan. The latter country has never enjoyed a good reputation among travellers; and Madame Pfeiffer's experience was not calculated to retrieve its character.

The caravan was crossing a corn-field which had been recently reaped, when half-a-dozen stalwart Kurds, armed with stout cudgels, sprang out from their hiding-place among the sheaves, and seizing the travellers' bridles, poured out upon them what was unmistakably a volley of oaths and threats. One of the travellers leaped from his steed, seized his assailant by the throat, and holding a loaded pistol to his head, indicated his determination of blowing out his brains. The effect of this resolute conduct was immediate; the robbers desisted from their attack, and were soon engaged in quite an amicable conversation with those they had intended to plunder. At last they pointed out a good place for an encampment, receiving in return a trifling *backshish*, collected from the whole caravan.

A few days later, the travellers, having started at two in the morning, entered a magnificent mountain-valley, which had been cloven through the solid rock by the waters of a copious stream. A narrow stony path followed the course of the stream upward. The moon shone in unclouded light; or it would have been difficult even for the well-trained horses of the caravan to have kept their footing along the dangerous way, encumbered as it was with fallen masses of rock.

Like chamois, however, they scrambled up the steep mountain-side, and safely carried their riders round frightful projections and past dangerous, dizzy precipices. So wild, so romantic was the scene, with its shifting lights and shadows, its sudden bursts of silvery lustre where the valley lay open to the moon, and its depths of darkness in many a winding recess, that even Madame Pfeiffer's uncultured companions were irresistibly moved by its influence; and as they rode along not a sound was heard but the clatter of the horses' hoofs, and the fall of rolling stones into the chasm below. But all at once thick clouds gathered over the moon, and the gloom became so intense that the travellers could scarcely discern each one his fellow. The leader continually struck fire with a flint, that the sparks might afford some slight indication of the proper course. But this was not enough; and as the horses began to miss their footing, the only hope of safety consisted in remaining immovable. With the break of day, however, a gray light spread over the scene, and the travellers found themselves surrounded by a circle of lofty mountains, rising one above the other in magnificent gradation, and superbly dominated by one mighty snow-crowned mass.

The journey was resumed. Soon the travellers became aware of the fact that the path was sprinkled with spots of blood. At last they came to a place which was crimsoned by a complete pool; and looking down into the ravine, they could see two human bodies, one lying scarcely a hundred feet below them, the other, which had rolled further, half hidden by a projecting crag. From this scene of murder they gladly hastened.

* * * * *

At a town called Ravandus Madame Pfeiffer rested for some days, making observations on the manners and customs of the Kurds. She was not prepossessed in their favour by what she saw: the women are idle, ignorant, and squalid; the men work as little and rob as much as they can. Polygamy is practised; and religion is reduced to the performance of a few formalities. The costume of the wealthier Kurds is purely Oriental, that of the common people varies from it a little. The men wear wide linen trousers, and over them a shirt confined by a girdle, with a sleeveless woollen jacket, made of stuff of only a hand's-breadth wide, and sewed together. Instead of white trousers, some wear brown, which are anything but picturesque, and look like sacks with two holes for the insertion of the feet,—the said feet being encased in boots of red or yellow leather, with large iron heels; or in shoes of coarse white wool, adorned with three tassels. The turban is the universal head-covering.

The women don loose trousers, and red or yellow boots, with iron heels, like the men; but over all they wear a long blue garment which, if not tucked up under the girdle, would depend some inches below the ankles. A large blue shawl descends below the knee. Round their heads they twist black shawls, turban-wise; or they wear the red fez, with a silk handkerchief wound about it; and on the top of this, a kind of wreath made of short black fringe, worn like a diadem, but leaving the forehead free. The hair falls in narrow braids over the shoulders, and from the turban droops a heavy silver chain. As a head-dress it is remarkably attractive; and it is but just to say that it often sets off really handsome faces, with fine features, and glowing eyes.

TARTAR CARAVAN.

* * * * *

In her further wanderings through the wild lands of Persia, our traveller came to Urumiyeh, on the borders of the salt lake of that name, which in several physical features closely resembles the Dead Sea. Urumiyeh is a place of some celebrity, for it gave birth to Zoroaster, the preacher of a creed of considerable moral purity, which has spread over a great part of Asia. Entering a more fertile country, she reached Tabreez in safety, and was once more within the influence of law and order. Tabreez, the residence of the viceroy, is a handsomely-built town, with numerous silk and leather manufactories, and is reputed to be one of the chief seats of Asiatic commerce. Its streets are clean and tolerably broad; in each a little rivulet is carried underground, with openings at regular intervals for the purpose of dipping out water. Of the houses the passer-by sees no more than is seen in any other Oriental town: lofty walls, windowless, with low entrances; and the fronts always looking in upon the open courtyards, which bloom with trees and flowers, and usually adjoin a pleasant garden. Inside, the chambers are usually lofty and spacious, with rows of windows which seem to form complete walls of glass. Buildings of public importance there are none; excepting the bazaar, which covers a considerable area, and is laid out with lofty, broad, and covered thoroughfares.

The traveller turned her back upon Tabreez on the 11th of August, and in a carriage drawn by post-horses, and attended by a single servant, set out for Natschivan. At Arax she crossed the frontier of Asiatic Russia, the dominions of the "White Tsar," who, in Asia as in Europe, is ever pressing more and more closely on the "unspeakable Turk." At Natschivan she joined a caravan which was bound for Tiflis, and the drivers of which were Tartars. She says of the latter, that they do not live so frugally as the Arabs. Every evening a savoury pillau was made with good-tasting fat, frequently with dried grapes or plums. They also partook largely of fruits.

The caravan wound through the fair and fertile valleys which lie at the base of Ararat. Of that famous and majestic mountain, which lifts its white glittering crest of snow some sixteen thousand feet above the sea-level, our traveller obtained a fine view. Its summit is cloven into two peaks, and in the space between an old tradition affirms that Noah's ark landed at the subsidence of the Great Flood.

MOUNT ARARAT.

In the neighbourhood of a town called Sidin, Madame Pfeiffer met with a singular adventure. She was returning from a short walk, when, hearing the sound of approaching post-horses, she paused for a minute to see the travellers, and noticed a Russian, seated in an open car, with a Cossack holding a musket by his side. As soon as the vehicle had passed, she resumed her course; when, to her astonishment, it suddenly stopped, and almost at the same moment she felt a fierce grasp on her arms. It was the

Cossack, who endeavoured to drag her to the car. She struggled with him, and pointing to the caravan, said she belonged to it; but the fellow put his hand on her mouth, and flung her into the car, where she was firmly seized by the Russian. Then the Cossack sprang to his seat, and away they went at a smart gallop. The whole affair was the work of a few seconds, so that Madame Pfeiffer could scarcely recognize what had happened. As the man still held her tightly, and kept her mouth covered up, she was unable to give an alarm. The brave woman, however, retained her composure, and speedily arrived at the conclusion that her "heroic" captors had mistaken her for some dangerous spy. Uncovering her mouth, they began to question her closely; and Madame Pfeiffer understood enough Russian to tell them her name, native country, and object in travelling. This did not satisfy them, and they asked for her passport,—which, however, she could not show them, as it was in her portmanteau.

At length they reached the post-house. Madame Pfeiffer was shown into a room, at the door of which the Cossack stationed himself with his musket. She was detained all night; but the next morning, having fetched her portmanteau, they examined her passport, and were then pleased to dismiss her—without, however, offering any apology for their shameful treatment of her. Such are the incivilities to which travellers in the Russian dominions are too constantly exposed. It is surprising that a powerful government should condescend to so much petty fear and mean suspicion.

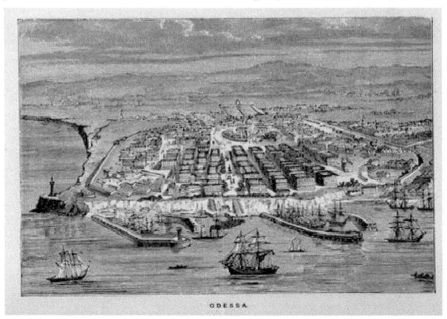

ODESSA.

From Tiflis our traveller proceeded across Georgia to Redutkali; whence she made her way to Kertsch, on the shore of the Sea of Azov; and thence to Sebastopol, destined a few years later to become the scene of an historic struggle. She afterwards reached Odessa, one of the great granaries of Europe, situated at the mouth of the Dniester and the Dnieper. From Odessa to Constantinople the distance by sea is four hundred and twenty miles. She made but a short stay in the Turkish capital; and then proceeded by steamer to Smyrna, passing through the maze of the beautiful isles of Greece; and from Smyrna to Athens. Here she trod on hallowed ground. Every temple, every ruin, recalled to her some brave deed of old, or some illustrious name of philosopher, warrior, statesman, poet, that the world will not willingly let die. A rush of stirring glorious memories swept over her mind as she gazed on the lofty summit of the Acropolis, covered with memorials of the ancient art, and associated with the great events of Athenian history. The Parthenon, or Temple of Pallas; the Temple of Theseus; that of Olympian Jove; the Tower of the Winds, or so-called Lantern of Demosthenes; and the Choragic Monument of Lysicrates,—all these she saw, and wondered at. But they have been so frequently described, that we may pass them here with this slight reference.

From Corinth our traveller crossed to Corfu, and from Corfu ascended the Adriatic to Trieste. A day or two afterwards she was received by her friends at Vienna,—having accomplished the most extraordinary journey ever undertaken by a woman, and made the complete circuit of the world. In the most remarkable scenes, and in the most critical positions, she had preserved a composure, a calmness of courage, and a simplicity of conduct, that must always command our admiration.

CHAPTER III.—NORTHWARD.

In giving to the world a narrative of her journey to Iceland, and her wanderings through Norway and Sweden, Madame Pfeiffer anticipated certain objections that would be advanced by the over-refined. "Another journey!" she supposed them to exclaim; "and that to regions far more likely to repel than attract the general traveller! What object could this woman have had in visiting them, but a desire to excite our astonishment and raise our curiosity? We might have been induced to pardon her pilgrimage to the Holy Land, though it was sufficiently hazardous for a solitary woman, because it was prompted, perhaps, by her religious feelings,—and incredible things, as we all know, are frequently accomplished under such an impulse. But, for the present expedition, what reasonable motive can possibly be suggested?"

Madame Pfeiffer remarks that in all this a great injustice is, or would be, done to her; that she was a plain, inoffensive creature, and by no means desirous of drawing upon herself the observation of the crowd. As a matter of fact, she was but following the bent of her natural disposition. From her earliest childhood she had yearned to go forth into the wide world. She could never meet a travelling-carriage without stopping to watch it, and envying the postilion who drove it or the persons it conveyed. When she was ten or twelve years old, no reading had such a charm for her as books of voyages and travels; and then she began to repine at the happiness of every great navigator or discoverer, whose boldness revealed to him the secrets of lands and seas before unknown.

She travelled much with her parents, and afterwards with her husband, and thus her natural bias was encouraged. It was not until her two sons were of age to be educated that she remained stationary—on their account. As the business concerns of her husband required his presence alternately in Vienna and in Lemberg, he intrusted to his wife the responsible duty of superintending their education—feeling assured that, with her perseverance and affection, she could supply the place of both parents.

When this duty was discharged, and the education of her sons completed, the dreams and fancies of her youth once more revived within her. She thought of the manners and customs of foreign lands, of remote islands girdled by the "melancholy main," and dwelt so long on the great joy of treading "the blessed acres" trodden by the Saviour's feet, that at last she resolved on a pilgrimage thither. She made the journey to Palestine. She visited Jerusalem, and other hallowed scenes, and she returned in safety. She came, therefore, to the conclusion that she was not presumptuously tempting the providence of God, or laying herself open to the charge of wishing to excite the admiration of her contemporaries, if she followed her inward impulse, and once more adventured forth to see the world. She knew that travel could not but broaden her views, elevate her thoughts, and inspire her with new sympathies. Iceland, the next object of her desires, was a country where she hoped to see Nature under an entirely novel and peculiar aspect. "I feel," she says, "so wonderfully happy, and draw so close to my Maker, while gazing upon such scenes, that no difficulties or fatigues can deter me from seeking so great a reward."

* * * * *

It was in the year 1845 that Madame Pfeiffer began her northward journey. She left Vienna on the 10th of April, and by way of Prague, Dresden, and Altona, proceeded to Kiel. Thence the steamer carried her to Copenhagen, a city of which she speaks in favourable terms. She notices its numerous splendid palaces; its large and regular squares; its broad and handsome promenades. At the Museum of Art she was interested by the chair which Tycho Brahe, the astronomer, formerly used; and at the Thorvaldsen Museum, the colossal lion executed by the great Danish sculptor. Having seen all that was to be seen, she took ship for Iceland, passing Helsingborg on the Swedish coast, and Elsinore on the Danish, the latter associated with Shakespeare's "Hamlet;" and, through the Sound and the Cattegat, entering upon the restless waters of the North Sea. Iceland came in sight on the seventh day of a boisterous voyage, which had tried our traveller somewhat severely; and at the close of the eleventh day she reached Havenfiord, an excellent harbour, two miles from Reikiavik, the capital of Iceland.

Her first impressions of the Icelandic coast, she says, were very different from the descriptions she had read in books. She had conceived of a barren desolate waste, shrubless and treeless; and she saw grassy hillocks, leafy copses, and even, as she thought, patches of dwarfish woods. But as she drew nearer, and could distinguish the different objects more plainly, the hillocks were transformed into human habitations, with small doors and windows; and the groups of trees proved to be huge lava masses, from ten to fifteen feet in height, entirely overgrown with verdure and moss. Everything was new, was surprising; and it was with pleasurable sensations of excitement and curiosity that Madame Pfeiffer landed on the shores of Ultima Thule.

REIKIAVIK

* * * * *

At Reikiavik she found the population inhabiting two very different classes of habitations. The wooden houses of the well-to-do are of a single story, she says, with five or six windows in front. A low flight of steps conducts to an entrance in the centre of the building; and this entrance opens into a vestibule, where two doors communicate with the rooms on the right and left respectively. In the rear is the kitchen, and beyond the courtyard. Such a house contains four or five rooms on the ground-floor, and a few small chambers under the roof. The domestic or household arrangements are entirely European. The furniture, much of which is mahogany, comes from Copenhagen, which also supplies the mirrors and cast-iron stoves. Handsome rugs are spread in front of the sofas; neat curtains drop before the windows; English engravings ornament the whitewashed walls; and china, silver, and cut-glass, and the like, are displayed upon the cabinets or corner-tables.

But the poor live in huts which are decidedly much more Icelandic. They are small and low; built of lava blocks, filled in with earth; and as the whole is covered with turf, they might almost be mistaken for natural elevations of the ground, if the wooden chimneys, and low doors, and almost imperceptible windows, did not betray that they were tenanted by human beings. A dark, narrow passage, not more than four feet high, leads on one hand to the living-room, on the other to the store-room, where the provisions are kept, and where, in winter, the cows and sheep are stabled.

The fireplace is generally at the end of this passage, which is purposely built low to keep out the cold. Neither the walls nor floors of these huts are boarded; the dwelling-rooms are scarcely large enough for people to sleep in or turn round in; and the whole furniture consists of the bedsteads (very poorly supplied with bedding), a small table, and a few chests—the latter, as well as the beds, being used for seats. To poles fastened in the walls are suspended clothes, shoes, stockings, and other articles; and in each hut is generally found a tiny book-shelf supporting a few volumes. No stoves are needed in these rooms, which are sufficiently warmed by the presence of their numerous inmates.

Speaking of the better classes of the inhabitants of the Icelandic capital, our traveller says: "Nothing struck me so much as the great dignity of carriage at which the Icelandic ladies aim, and which is so apt to degenerate into stiffness when it is not perfectly natural, or has not become a second nature by habit. They incline their head very coolly when you meet them, with less civility than we should use towards an inferior or a stranger. The lady of the house never accompanies her guests beyond the door of the room, after a call; if the husband is present, he goes a little further; but when this is not the case, you are often at a loss which way to turn, as there is no servant on the spot to open the street door for you, unless it may happen to be in the house of the Stiftsamtmann, the first dignitary of the island."

The church at Reikiavik is capable of accommodating about one hundred and fifty persons; it is built of stone, with a wooden roof, under which is kept a library of several thousand volumes. It possesses an artistic treasure of no ordinary value in a font by Thorvaldsen, whose parents were natives of Iceland, though he himself was born in Denmark. Captain Burton describes it as the ancient classical altar, with basso-relievos on all four sides—subjects of course evangelical; on the top an alto-relievo of symbolical flowers, roses, and passifloræ is cut to support the normal "Dobefal," or baptismal basin. In the sacristy are preserved some handsome priestly robes—especially the velvet vestment sent by Pope Julius II. to the last Roman Catholic bishop in the early part of the sixteenth century, and still worn by the chief Protestant dignitary at ordinations.

The climate at Reikiavik would be considered severe by an Englishman. The thermometer sometimes sinks as low as 13° below zero, and the sea is covered with ice for several feet from the shore. The storms and snow-drifts are of the most terrible character, and at times even the boldest Icelander dares not cross his threshold. Daylight does not last more than four or five hours; but the long night is illuminated by the splendid coruscations of the aurora, filling the firmament with many-coloured flame. From the middle until the end of June, however, there is no night.

The sun sinks for a short time below the hills, but twilight blends with the dawn, and before the last rays of evening have faded from the sky the morning light streams forth with renewed brilliancy.

* * * * *

Then, as to the people, Madame Pfeiffer speaks of them as of medium height and strength. Their hair is light, and frequently has a reddish tint; their eyes are blue. The women are more prepossessing in appearance than the men; and pleasing faces are not uncommon among the young girls. They wear long skirts of coarse black woollen stuff, with spencers, and coloured aprons. They cover their heads with a man's cap of the same material as their petticoats, ending in a drooping point, to which hangs a woollen or silken tassel, falling as low as the shoulders. This simple head-dress is not inelegant. All the women have an abundance of hair hanging picturesquely about their face and neck; they wear it loose and short, and it is sometimes curled.

The men appear to dress very much like the German peasants. They wear pantaloons, jackets, and vests of dark cloth, with a felt hat or fur cap, and the feet wrapped in pieces of skin, either seal, sheep, or calf.

* * * * *

Here, as a corrective, and for the sake of comparison, let us refer to Captain Burton's description. The men dress, he says, like sailors, in breeches, jackets serving as coats, and vests of good broadcloth, with four to six rows of buttons, always metal, either copper or silver. The fishermen wear overcoats, coarse smooth waistcoats, large paletots, made waterproof by grease or fish-liver oil; leather overalls, stockings, and native shoes. The women attire themselves in jackets and gowns, petticoats and aprons of woollen frieze; over which is thrown a "hempa," or wide black robe, like a Jesuit frock, trimmed with velvet binding. The wealthy add silver ornaments down the length of the dress, and braid the other articles with silk ribbons, galloon, or velvets of various colours. The ruff forms a stiff collar, from three to four inches broad, of very fine stuff, embroidered with gold or silver. The conical head-dress, resembling a fool's-cap or sugar-loaf, measures two or three feet high, and is kept in its place by a coarse cloth, and covered with a finer kerchief. The soleless shoes of ox-hide or sheepskin, made by the women out of a single piece, are strapped to the instep.

* * * * *

Having made herself generally acquainted with the Icelanders and their mode of living, Madame Pfeiffer began to visit the most romantic and interesting spots in the island accessible to an adventurous woman. At first she confined herself to the neighbourhood of Reikiavik. She journeyed, for instance, to the island of Vidöe, the cliffs of which are frequented by the eider-duck. Its tameness while brooding is very remarkable. "I had always looked," she says, "on the wonderful stories I had heard on this subject as fabulous, and should do still had I not been an eye-witness to the fact. I approached and laid my hands on the birds while they were sitting; yes, I could even caress them without their attempting to move from their nests; or, if they left them for a moment, it was only to walk off for a few steps, and remain quietly waiting till I withdrew, when they immediately returned to their station. Those whose young were already hatched, however, would beat their wings with violence, and snap at me with their bills when I came near them, rather allowing themselves to be seized than to desert their broods. In size they resemble our common duck; their eggs are of a greenish-gray, rather larger than hens' eggs, and of an excellent flavour. Each bird lays about eleven eggs. The finest down is that with which they line their nests at first; it is of a dark gray, and is regularly carried off by the islanders with the first eggs. The poor bird then robs itself of a second portion of its down, and lays a few more eggs, which are also seized; and it is not till the nest has been felted for the third time that the ducks are left unmolested to bring up their brood. The down of the second, and particularly that of the third hatching, is much lighter than the first, and of an inferior quality."

The salmon-fishery at the Larsalf next engaged our traveller's attention. It is conducted after a primitively simple fashion. When the fish at spawning-time seek the quiet waters of the inland stream, their way back to the sea is blocked up by an embankment of loose stones, about three feet high. In front of this wall is extended a net; and several similar barriers are erected at intervals of eighty to a hundred paces, to prevent the fish which have slipped over one of them from finally accomplishing their escape. A day is appointed for a grand *battue*. The water is then let off as much as possible; and the ensnared fish, feeling it grow shallower, dart hither and thither in frantic confusion, and eventually gather together in such a mass that the fishermen have only to thrust in their hands and seize their prey.

Yet *some* degree of skill is necessary, for, as everybody knows, the salmon is full of vivacity, and both strong and swift. So the fisher takes his victim dexterously by head and tail, and throws it ashore immediately. It is caught up by persons who are specially appointed to this duty, and flung to a still greater distance from the stream. Were not this done, and done quickly, many a fine fellow would escape. It is strange to see the fish turn round in the hands of their captors, and leap into the air, so that if the fishermen were not provided with woollen mittens, they could not keep their hold of the slippery creatures at all. In these wholesale razzias, from five hundred to a thousand fish are generally taken at a time, each one weighing from five to fifteen pounds.

SALMON-FISHING IN ICELAND.

* * * * *

Iceland may, with little exaggeration, be described as nothing more than a stratum of snow and ice overlying a mass of fire and vapour and boiling water. Nowhere else do we see the two elements of frost and fire in such immediate contiguity. The icy plains are furrowed by lower currents, and in the midst of wastes of snow rise the seething ebullitions of hot springs. Several of the snow-shrouded mountains of Iceland are volcanic. In the neighbourhood of Kriservick Madame Pfeiffer saw a long, wide valley, traversed by a current of lava, half a mile in length; a current consisting not merely of isolated blocks and stones, but of large masses of porous rock, ten or twelve feet high, frequently broken up by fissures a foot wide.

Six miles further, and our traveller entered another valley, where, from the sulphur-springs and hills, rose numerous columns of smoke. Ascending the neighbouring hills, she saw a truly remarkable scene: basins filled with bubbling waters, and vaporous shafts leaping up from the fissures in the hills and plains. By keeping to windward, she was able to approach very near these phenomenal objects; the ground was lukewarm in a few places, and she could hold her hand for several minutes at a time over the cracks whence the vapour escaped. No water was visible. The roar and hiss of the steam, combined with the violence of the wind, made a noise so deafening that she was glad to quit the scene, and feel a safer soil beneath her feet. It seemed to her excited fancy as if the entire mountain were converted into a boiling caldron.

Descending into the plain, she found there much to interest her. Here a basin was filled with boiling mud; there, from another basin, burst forth a column of steam with fearful violence. Several hot springs bubbled and bubbled around. "These spots," says our traveller, "were far more dangerous than any on the hills; in spite of the utmost caution, we often sank in above our ankles, and drew back our feet in dread, covered with the damp exhalations, which, with steam or boiling water, also escaped from the opening. I allowed my guide to feel his way in front of me with a stick; but, notwithstanding his precaution, he went through in one place half-way to his knee—though he was so used to the danger that he treated it very lightly, and stopped quite phlegmatically at the next spring to cleanse himself from the mud. Being also covered with it to the ankles, I followed his example."

* * * * *

We must now accompany our traveller on some longer excursions.

And first, to Thingvalla, the place where, of old, the Althing or island-parliament was annually held. One side of the great valley of council is bounded by the sea, the other by a fine range of peaks, always more or less covered with snow. Through the pass of the Almannagja we descend upon the Thingvallavatn lake, an expanse of placid blue, about thirty miles in circuit. While our attention is rivetted on the lake and the dark brown hills which encircle it, a chasm suddenly, and as if by enchantment, opens at our feet, separating us from the valleys beyond. It varies from thirty to forty feet in width, is several hundred feet in depth, and four miles in length.

"We were compelled," says Madame Pfeiffer, "to descend its steep and dangerous sides by a narrow path leading over fragments of lava. My uneasiness increased as we went down, and could see the colossal masses, in the shape of pillars or columns tottering loosely on the brink of the precipice above our heads, threatening death and desolation at any moment. Mute and anxious, we crept along in breathless haste, scarcely venturing to raise our eyes, much less to give vent to the least expression of alarm, for fear of starting the avalanche of stone, of the impetuous force of which we could form some idea by the shattered rocks around us. The echo is very remarkable, and gives back the faintest whisper with perfect distinctness."

* * * * *

Every traveller to Iceland feels bound to visit its Geysirs, and Madame Pfeiffer did as others did. From Thingvalla she rode for some distance along the side of the lakes, and then struck through a rocky pass of a very difficult character, into a series of valleys of widely different aspect. At last she came to a stream which flowed over a bed of lava, and between banks of lava, with great rapidity and a rushing, roaring sound. At one point the river-bed was cleft through its centre, to the depth of eighteen or twenty feet, by a chasm from fifteen to eighteen feet wide, into which the waters pour with considerable violence. A bridge in the middle of the river spans this rift, and the stranger who reaches the banks feels unable to account for its appearance among the cloud of spray which entirely conceals the chasm in the bed of the stream.

Into her description of the passage of the river it is to be feared that Madame Pfeiffer introduces a little exaggeration. The waters roar, she says, with the utmost violence, and dashing wildly into the cavity, they form falls on both sides of it, or shiver themselves to spray against the projecting cliffs; at the extremity of the chasm, which is not far from the bridge, the stream is precipitated in its whole breadth over rocks from thirty to forty feet in height. "Our horses began to tremble, and struggled to escape when we drew near the most furious part of the torrent, where the noise was really deafening; and it was not without the greatest difficulty we succeeded in making them obey the reins, and bear us through the foaming waves by which the bridge was washed." Either the scene has greatly altered since Madame Pfeiffer's visit, or her imagination has considerably over-coloured its principal features. That is, if we accept the accounts of recent travellers, and especially that of Captain Burton, who has laboured so successfully to reduce the romance of Icelandic travel to plain matter of fact.

GREAT GEYSIR.

The Geysirs lie within a comparatively limited area, and consist of various specimens, differing considerably in magnitude. The basin of the Great Geysir lies on a gentle elevation, about ten feet above the plain; it measures about one hundred and fifty feet in diameter, while that of the seething caldron is ten feet. Both caldron and basin, on the occasion of Madame Pfeiffer's visit, were full to the brim with crystal-clear water in a state of slight ebullition. At irregular intervals a column of water is shot perpendicularly upwards from the centre of the caldron, the explosion being always preceded by a low rumbling; but she was not so fortunate as to witness one of these eruptions. Lord Dufferin, however, after three days' watch, was rewarded for his patience. The usual underground thunder having been heard, he and his friends rushed to the spot. A violent agitation was convulsing the centre of the pool. Suddenly a crystal dome lifted itself up to the height of eight or ten feet, and then fell; immediately after which, a shining liquid column, or rather a sheaf of columns, wreathed in robes of vapour, sprang into the air, and in a succession of jerking leaps, each higher than its predecessor, flung their silver crests against the sky.

For a few minutes the fountain held its own, then all at once appeared to lose its ascending power. The unstable waters faltered, drooped, fell, "like a broken purpose," back upon themselves, and were immediately absorbed in the depths of the subterranean shaft.

About one hundred and forty yards distant is the Strokkr, or "churn," with a basin about seven feet wide in its outer, and eighteen feet in its inner diameter. A funnel or inverted cone in shape, whereas the Great Geysir is a mound and a cylinder, it gives the popular idea of a crater. Its surface is "an ugly area of spluttering and ever boiling water." It frequently "erupts," and throws a spout into the air, sometimes as high as forty or fifty feet, the outbursts lasting from ten to thirty minutes. Madame Pfeiffer had not the luck to see it in its grandest moods; the highest eruption she saw did not rise above thirty feet, nor last more than fifteen minutes. An eruption can be produced by throwing into the caldron a sufficient quantity of turf or stones.

Two remarkable springs lie directly above the Geysirs, in openings separated by a barrier of rock—which, however, rise nowhere above the level of the ground. Their waters boil very gently, with an equable and almost rhythmic flow. The charm of these springs lies in their wonderful transparency and clearness. All the prominent points and corners, the varied outlines of the cavities, and the different recesses, can be distinguished far within the depths, until the eye is lost in the darkness of the abyss; and the luminous effects upon the rocks lend an additional beauty to the scene, which has all the magic of the poet's fairy-land. It is illumined by a radiance of a soft pale blue and green, which reaches only a few inches from the rocky barrier, leaving the waters beyond in colourless transparency. The light, to all appearance, seems reflected from the rock, but is really owing to atmospheric causes.

* * * * *

From the Geysirs, Madame Pfeiffer proceeded towards Hekla; and at the village of Thorfüstadir, on the route, had an opportunity of seeing an Icelandic funeral. On entering the church she found the mourners consoling themselves with a dram of brandy. On the arrival of the priest, a psalm or prayer was screamed, under his direction, by a chosen number of the congregation; each shouting his loudest, until he was completely out of breath. The priest, standing by the coffin, which, for lack of better accommodation, was resting on one of the seats, read in a loud voice a prayer of more than half an hour's duration. The body was then borne to the grave, which was one of remarkable depth; and the coffin being duly lowered, the priest threw earth upon it thrice, thus terminating the ceremony.

At the little village of Skalholt, where the first Icelandic bishopric was established in 1095, Madame Pfeiffer was invited to visit the church, and inspect its treasures. She was shown the grave of the first bishop, Thorlakúr, whose memory is cherished as that of a saint; an old embroidered robe, and a plain gold chalice, both of which probably belonged to him; and, in an antique chest, some dusty books in the Iceland dialect, besides three ponderous folios in German, containing the letters, epistles, and treatises of Martin Luther.

Continuing her journey, she arrived at the little village of Sälsun, which lies at the foot of Mount Hekla. Here she secured the services of a guide, and made preparations for the ascent of the famous volcano. These included the purchase of a store of bread and cheese, and the supply of a bottle of water for herself, and one of brandy for the guide, besides long sticks, shod with iron, to steady the adventurers' footsteps.

The day fixed for the expedition opened brightly and warmly. At first the road led through fields of tolerable fertility, covered with a rich green herbage, soft as velvet; and then traversed patches of black sand, surrounded by hills, and blocks, and currents of lava. By degrees it grew more difficult, and was so encumbered with lava as greatly to impede the progress of the travellers. Around and behind them rolled the dark congealed lava; and it was needful to be constantly on the watch, to prevent themselves from stumbling, or to avoid rude contact with the rolling rocks. Greater still was the danger in the rifts and gorges filled with snow moistening already in the summer heat; here they frequently broke through the deceptive crust, or at every step slipped backwards almost as far as they had advanced.

MOUNT HEKLA

At length they reached a point where it became necessary to leave behind the horses, and trust entirely to their own strength. Laboriously, but undauntedly, Madame Pfeiffer pressed upward. Yet, as she looked around on the sterile scene, which seemed to have been swept by a blast of fire, and on the drear expanse of black lava that surrounded her, Madame Pfeiffer could scarcely repress a sensation of pain and terror.

They had still, she says, three heights to climb; the last of which was also the most dangerous. The path clambered up the rocks which covered the entire area of the mountain-summit. Frequent were our traveller's falls; her hands were sadly wounded by the sharp jagged projections of the lava; and her eyes suffered severely from the dazzling brilliancy of the snow that filled every gorge and ravine.

But every obstacle gives way to the resolute; and at last Madame Pfeiffer stood on the topmost peak of Hekla. Here she made a discovery: in books of travel she had read of the crater of Mount Hekla, but a careful survey convinced her that none existed. There was neither opening, crevasse, nor sunken wall; in fact, no sign of a crater. Lower down on the mountain-side she detected some wide fissures; and from these, not from any crater, must have rolled the lava-rivers. The height of the mountain is computed at 5110 feet.

During the last hour of the ascent the sun had been veiled in mists, and from the neighbouring glaciers dense clouds now poured down upon them, obscuring or concealing the entire prospect. Fortunately, they gradually dissolved into snow, which spread a carpet, white and soft and glittering, over the dreary lava. The thermometer stood at 29¾° F.

The snow-storm passed, and the sun once more gladdened earth, and filled with light the clear blue arch of the firmament. On her elevated watchtower stood the adventurous traveller, till the clouds, passing away, opened up to her wondering gaze the glorious view—glorious, yet terrible! It seemed as if the ruins of a burned-up world lay all around: the wastes were strewn with masses of lava; of life not a sign was visible; blocks of barren lava were piled upon one another in chaotic confusion; and vast streams of indurated volcanic matter choked up every valley.

"Here, on the topmost peak of Hekla," writes Madame Pfeiffer, "I could look down far and wide upon the uninhabited land, the image of a torpid nature, passionless, inanimate, and yet sublime,—an image which, once seen, can never be forgotten, and the remembrance of which will compensate me amply for all the toils and difficulties I have endured. A whole world of glaciers, lava-peaks, fields of snow and ice, rivers and miniature lakes, were comprehended in that magnificent prospect; and the foot of man had never yet ventured within these regions of gloom and solitude. How terrible must have been the resistless fury of the element which has produced all these changes! And is its rage now silenced for ever? Will it be satisfied with the ruin it has wrought? Or does it slumber only to break forth again with renewed strength, and lay waste those few cultivated spots which are scattered so sparingly throughout the land? I thank God that he has allowed me to see this chaos of his creation; and I doubly thank him that my lot was cast in these fair plains where the sun does more than divide the day from the night; where it warms and animates plant-life and animal-life; where it awakens in the heart of man the deepest feelings of gratitude towards his Maker."

On her way down our traveller discovered that the snow had not melted for the first five or six hundred feet. Below that distance the mountain-sides were enveloped in a shroud of vapour. That glossy, coal-black, shining lava, which is never porous, can be found only at Hekla and in its immediate vicinity; but the other varieties, jagged, porous, and vitrified, are also met with, though they are invariably black, as is the sand which covers the side of the mountain. As the distance from the volcano increases, the lava loses its jet-black colour, and fades into an iron-gray.

After an absence of twelve hours, Madame Pfeiffer reached Sälsun in safety.

Six-and-twenty eruptions of Hekla have been recorded,—the last having occurred in 1845-46. One was prolonged for a period of six years, spreading desolation over a country which had formerly been the seat of a prosperous settlement, and burying the cultivated fields beneath a flood of lava, scoriæ, and ashes. During the eruption of 1845-46, three new crater-vents were formed, from which sprang columns of fire and smoke to the height of 14,000 feet. The lava accumulated in formidable masses, and fragments of scoriæ and pumice-stone weighing two hundredweight were thrown to a distance of a league and a half; while the ice and snow which had lain on the mountain for centuries were liquefied, and rolled in devastating torrents over the plains.

Hekla is not the only volcanic mountain of Iceland. Mounts Leirhnukr and Krabla, in the northeast, are very formidable; and one of the most terrible eruptions recorded in the island annals was that of the Skaptá Jokul in 1783.

We have now completed our summary of Madame Pfeiffer's Icelandic excursions. From the country we may pass to its inhabitants, and ascertain the deliberate opinion she had formed of them after an experience extending over several weeks, and under conditions which enabled so shrewd an observer as she was to judge them impartially. Her estimate of their character is decidedly less favourable than that of her predecessors; but it is to be noted that in almost every particular it is confirmed by the latest authority, Captain Burton. And the evidence goes to show that they are not the simple, generous, primitive, guileless Arcadians which it had pleased some fanciful minds to portray.

Their principal occupation consists in the fisheries, which are pursued with the greatest activity during the months of February, March, and April. The people from the interior then stream into the different harbours, and bargain with the coast-population, the fishermen proper, to help them for a share of the profits. On the other hand, in July and August many of the coast-population penetrate inland, and lend their services in the hay-harvest, for which they are paid in butter, wool, and salted lamb. Others resort to the mountains in search of Iceland moss, which they mix with milk, and use as an article of food; or grind it into meal, and make cakes with it, as a substitute for bread. The labours of the women consist in preparing the fish for drying, smoking, or salting; in tending the cattle, in knitting, and gathering moss. During the winter season both men and women knit uninterruptedly.

Madame Pfeiffer thinks their hospitality has been overrated, and gives them credit for the ability to make a good bargain. In fact, she saw nothing of that disinterestedness which Dr. Henderson and other travellers have ascribed to them. They are intolerably addicted to brandy-drinking,—indeed, their circumstances would greatly improve if they drank less and worked more. They are scarcely less passionately addicted to snuff-taking, as well as to tobacco-chewing. Their mode of taking snuff is peculiar, and certainly not one to be imitated. Most of the peasants, and even many of the priests, have no snuff-boxes, but make use instead of a piece of bone, turned in the shape of a little powder-horn. When desirous of indulging in a little titillation, they throw back their heads, and putting the point of the horn to their nostril, empty in the snuff. So little fastidious are these devotees, that they frequently pass on a horn from nose to nose, without the needless formality of cleaning it. The mention of this practice leads Madame Pfeiffer to comment very severely on the want of cleanliness among the Icelanders, who are as dirty in their houses as in their persons.

They are also remarkable for their laziness. There are many ample stretches of meadow-land at a short distance from the coast, completely covered with bog, and passable only with great precautions, which the construction of a few ditches would thoroughly drain. Capital grass would then spring up in abundant crops. It is well known that such will grow in Iceland, for the hillocks which rise above the swamps are luxuriantly overgrown with herbage and wild clover. The best soil is found, it is said, on the north side of the island, where potatoes grow very well, and also a few trees—which, however, do not exceed seven or eight feet in height. The chief occupation of the northerners is cattle-breeding, particularly in the interior, where some of the farmers own three or four hundred sheep, ten or fifteen cows, and a dozen horses. These, it is true, are exceptional cases; but, as a rule, the population here are in much better circumstances than the wretched coast-population, who chiefly rely on the products of their fisheries.

* * * * *

From Iceland Madame Pfeiffer embarked for Copenhagen on the 29th of July, in the sloop *Haabet* (the "Hope"), which proved by no means a vessel of luxurious accommodation. Our resolute voyager gives an amusing account of her trials. The fare, for instance, was better adapted for a hermit than for a lady of gentle nurture; but it was sublimely impartial, being exactly the same for captain, mate, crew, and passengers. For breakfast they had wretched tea,—or rather, dirty tea-coloured water,—which the common hands drank without any sugar. The officers made use of a small lump of candy, holding it in their mouths, where it melted slowly, while they swallowed cup after cup to moisten the hard ship-biscuit and rancid butter.

The dinners, however, showed a daily variation. First, a piece of salted meat, which, having been soaked and boiled in sea-water, was so intolerably hard, tough, and salt that it required the digestion of an ostrich to overtake it. Instead of soup, vegetables, or dessert, barley grits were served up, plainly boiled, without salt or butter, and eaten with syrup and vinegar. On the second day, the *pièce de resistance* was a lump of bacon, boiled in salt water; this was followed by the barley grits. On the third day, cod-fish and pease; on the fourth, the same bill of fare as on the first; and so on,—a cup of coffee, without milk, closing the noonday meal. The evening's repast resembled that of the morning, consisting of tea-water and ship-biscuit.

So much for the fare. As to the "table appointments," they were miserably meagre. The cloth was a piece of an old sail, so soiled and dirty that it effectually deprived Madame Pfeiffer and her fellow-passengers of any small appetite with which they might have sat down to dinner. Madame Pfeiffer began to think that it would be better to have no cloth at all. She was mistaken! One day she saw the steward belabouring a piece of sailcloth, which was stretched on the deck under his feet, to receive a good sweeping from the ship's broom. The numerous spots of dirt and grease showed plainly that it was the table-cloth; and that same evening the table was bare. The consequence was, that the teapot had no sooner been placed upon it than it began to slide; and nothing but the captain's adroitness prevented the entire "bill of fare" from being poured into the laps of the guests. It then became evident that

> A table-cloth all foul and stained
> Is better far than none at all!

The *Hope* was twenty days at sea, and for twelve days out of sight of land. She was wind-driven to the westward, so that her passengers saw but few of the monsters of the Northern Seas. They caught sight of the spout of a single whale in the distance; it rose in the air exactly like a fountain-jet, but the animal itself was too far off for its huge outlines to be discernible. One shark had the gallantry to swim round them for a few minutes, affording them an opportunity of observing it closely. It appeared to be from sixteen to eighteen feet in length.

* * * * *

The "unresting" traveller reached Copenhagen on the 19th of August, and on the very same day embarked again for Sweden and Norway.

Let us accompany her to Christiania. This town and its suburbs, the fortress, the royal castle, the freemasons' lodge, and other buildings, surmount the noble harbour in a stately semicircle; which, in its turn, is enclosed by meadows, and woods, and green hills. As if loath to leave a scene so charming, the blue sea winds in among the fields and vales to some distance behind the town.

The best part of Christiania is, not unnaturally, the latest built, where the streets are broad and long, and the houses, both of brick and stone, substantial. In the suburbs, most of the houses are of timber. Some of the public edifices are architecturally conspicuous, particularly the new castle and the fortress, which are finely situated on a commanding elevation, and enjoy a prospect of great extent and splendid variety.

Madame Pfeiffer was much struck by the diverseness of the conveyances that dash through the pleasant, breezy streets of this picturesque city. The most common, but the least convenient, are called *carriols*. They consist of a very long, narrow, and uncovered box, strung between two enormously high wheels, and provided with a very small seat, into which the passenger must squeeze himself, with outstretched feet, and a leathern apron drawn over his legs; nor can he, nor dare he, move, from the moment he gets in until he gets out again. A place behind is provided for the coachman, in case the occupant of the *carriol* is disinclined to drive; but as it is unpleasant to have the reins shaken about one's head, and the whip constantly flourishing in one's ears, the services of a driver are seldom in requisition. Besides these unshapely vehicles, there are phaetons, droschkis, chariots, and similar light conveyances; but no covered carriages.

* * * * *

From Christiania to Stockholm.

At Gothenburg Madame Pfeiffer embarked on board the steamer which plies on the Götha Canal, the great water-way, linking streams and lakes, which affords access to the Swedish capital. She found herself before long on the River Götha, and at Lilla Edet came to the first of the five locks which occur there. While the boat was passing through them she had an opportunity of seeing the Götha Falls, which, though of no great height, pour down a considerable volume of water.

Through fir woods, brown with shadows, the canal winds onward to the magnificent locks of Trollhatten—an engineering achievement of which any nation might be justly proud. They are eleven in number, and rise by gradations to a height of 112 feet in a distance of 3550 feet. The wide, deep channel excavated in the rock is literally paved with flagstones; and these locks mount one above the other like the solitary steps of a majestic stairway, and almost lay claim to be ranked among the world's wonders.

While the steamer passes through the successive barriers the passengers have time to make an excursion to the falls of Trollhatten, which are less remarkable for their elevation than for their flood of waters and the picturesqueness of the surrounding scenery.

Beyond Trollhatten the stream expands to the proportions of a lake, while a number of green and wooded islands divide it into several channels. Thence it traverses the Lake of Wenner, which is ten or twelve miles long, and proceeds onward through a country of no great interest, until at

Sjotorp it passes into the river again. A few miles further, and it crosses the Vilkensoc, which, like all the other Swedish lakes, is charmingly studded with islands. It lies three hundred and six feet above the level of the North Sea, and is the culminating point of the canal, which thence descends through about seventy locks, traversing the Bottensee and Lake Wetter.

After a tedious journey of five days, Madame Pfeiffer reached the shores of the Baltic, which are finely indented by bays and rivers, with long stretches of lofty cliff, and, inland, dense masses of fir woods. Leaving the sea again, a short canal conducts the voyager into Lake Mälar, celebrated for its cluster of islands. The lake at first resembles a broad river, but soon widens to a great extent; the beauty of the scenery never fails to excite the traveller's admiration. It is said that a thousand isles besprinkle its surface; they are crowded together in the most picturesque and varied groups, forming streams, and bays, and a chain of smaller lakes, and continually revealing some new and attractive feature.

Not less charming the shores: sometimes the hills and mountains pass close to the water, and their steep and rocky sides frown like thunder-smitten ramparts; but generally the eye is delighted by a constant and brightly-coloured panorama of meadows, woods, and valleys, villages, and sequestered farmhouses. On the summit of a steep declivity a high pole is erected, to which hangs suspended the hat of the unfortunate King Erik. It is said of him, that having fled from the field of battle, he was here overtaken by one of his soldiers, whose stern reproaches so stung him to the heart that he drove his spurs into his horse's sides, and clearing the precipice with a bound, sank for ever beneath the waters of the lake. His hat, which fell from his head as he made the plunge, is preserved as a memorial of a king's remorse.

* * * * *

On arriving at Stockholm, several stalwart women offer us their services as porters. They are Dalecarlians, who earn a livelihood by carrying luggage or water, by rowing boats, and by resorting to other occupations generally reserved for the stronger sex. Honest, industrious, capable of immense fatigue, they never lack employment. They wear short black petticoats, red bodices, white chemises with long sleeves, short and narrow aprons of two colours, red stockings, and shoes with thick wooden soles. Around their heads they generally bind a handkerchief, or else wear a very small black cap, which just covers the back of their hair.

Stockholm proves, on examination, to be a handsome city, situated at the junction of the Baltic with the Lake Mälar; or, more strictly speaking, on the banks of a short canal which unites the two. One of its most conspicuous buildings is the stately Ritterholm Church, which Madame Pfeiffer describes as resembling rather a vault and an armoury than a religious edifice. In the side chapels are enshrined the monuments of dead Swedish kings, whose bones lie in the royal sepulchres below. On both sides of the nave are ranged the equestrian statues of armed knights; while from every vantage-point hang flags and standards. The keys of captured towns and fortresses are suspended in the side chapels, and drums and kettle-drums piled upon the floor—trophies won from the enemies of Sweden in the days when she was a great European power. The chapels also contain, enclosed in glass-cases, parts of the dress and armour of some of the Swedish monarchs. We notice, with keen interest, the uniform worn by Charles XII.—he

> "Who left a name at which the world grew pale,
> To point a moral or adorn a tale"—

at the time of his death, and the hat penetrated by the fatal shot that slew the fiery warrior. A remarkable contrast is afforded by the rich dress and plumed hat of Bernadotte, the French soldier of fortune, who founded the present royal house.

The royal palace is a stately structure, and its interior is enriched with the costliest decoration. The Ritter-house, the Museum of Ancient Art, the Crown-Prince's palace, the theatre, the bank, the mint, are all deserving of inspection. In the vicinity a trip may be made to the beautiful and diversified scenery of the Royal Park, or the military school at Karlberg, or to the ancient royal castle of Gripsholm on the Lake of Mälar.

But our last excursion must be directed, by way of Upsala, to the iron-mines of Danemora.

The little village of Danemora is embosomed in woods. It contains a small church and a few scattered houses of various dimensions. The neighbourhood abounds in the usual indications of a mining locality. Madame Pfeiffer arrived in what is called "the nick of time," and just opportunely, to witness the blasting of the ore. From the wide opening of the largest mine it is possible to see what passes below; and a strange and wonderful sight it is to peer down into the abyss, four hundred and eighty feet deep, and observe the colossal entrances to the various pits, the rocky bridges, the projections, arches, and caverns excavated in the solid rock. The miners appear so many puppets; their movements can hardly be distinguished, until the eye has grown accustomed to the darkness and to their diminutive size.

At the given moment a match was applied to four trains of gunpowder. The man who lighted them immediately sprang back, and hid himself behind a wall of rock. In a minute or two came the flash; a few stones were hurled into the air; and immediately afterwards was heard a loud detonation, and the shattered mass fell in fragments all around. Echo caught up the tremendous explosion, and carried it to the furthest recesses of the mine; while, to enhance the terror of the scene, one rock was hardly shivered before another crash was heard, and then a third, and immediately afterwards a fourth.

IRON-MINE OF DANEMORA.

The other pits are still deeper, one of them being six hundred feet beneath the ground; but as they are smaller in their openings, and as the shafts are not always perpendicular, the gaze is soon lost in the obscurity, which produces a dismal effect upon the spectator. The iron obtained from the Swedish mines is of excellent quality, and large quantities are annually exported.

* * * * *

Madame Pfeiffer now began her homeward journey, and, by way of Hamburg and Berlin, proceeded to Dresden. Thence she returned to Vienna on the 6th of October, after an absence of six months.

CHAPTER IV.—LAST TRAVELS.

Madame Pfeiffer set out on what proved to be her final expedition, on the 21st of May 1856. She proceeded to Berlin, thence to Amsterdam, Leyden, Rotterdam; visited London and Paris; and afterwards undertook the voyage to the Cape of Good Hope. Here she hesitated for a while in what direction she should turn her adventurous steps before she pushed forward to the goal of her hopes—Madagascar. At length she decided on a visit to the Mauritius; and it is at this part of her journey that we propose to take up her record.

PORT LOUIS, MAURITIUS.

She saw much scenery in this rich and beautiful little island that moved her to admiration. The volcanic mountains assume the boldest and most romantic outlines. The vegetation is of the most luxuriant character. Each deep gorge or mountain-valley blooms with foliage; and the slopes are clothed with stately trees, graceful shrubs, and climbing plants; while shining streams fall from crag to crag in miniature cascades. Of course Madame Pfeiffer visited the sugar-cane plantations, which cover the broad and fertile plains of Pamplemousse. She learned that the sugar-cane is not raised from seed, but that pieces of cane are planted. The first cane requires eighteen months to ripen; but as, meanwhile, the chief stem throws out shoots, each of the following harvests can be gathered in at intervals of twelve months; hence four crops can be obtained in four years and a half.

After the fourth harvest, the field must be cleared completely of the cane. If the land be virgin soil, on which no former crop has been raised, fresh slips of cane may be planted immediately, and thus eight crops secured in nine years. But if such is not the case, "ambrezades" must be planted— that is, a leafy plant, growing to the height of eight or nine feet, the leaves of which, continually falling, decay and fertilize the soil. After two years the plants are rooted out, and the ground is once more occupied by a sugar plantation.

When the canes are ripe and the harvest begins, every day as many canes are cut down as can be pressed and boiled at once. The cane is introduced between two rollers, set in motion by steam-power, and pressed until it is quite flat and dry: in this state it is used for fuel. The juice is strained successively into six pans, of which the first is exposed to the greatest heat—the force of the fire being diminished gradually under each of the others. In the last pan the sugar is found half crystallized. It is then deposited on great wooden tables to cool, and granulate into complete crystals of about the size of a pin's head. Lastly, it is poured into wooden colanders, to filter it thoroughly of the molasses it still contains. The whole process occupies eight or ten days. Before the sugar is packed, it is spread out on the open terraces to dry for some hours in the sun.

* * * * *

An excursion was made to Mount Orgueil, in order to obtain a panoramic view of the island-scenery. On one side the lofty ridge of the Morne Brabant, connected with the mainland only by a narrow neck of earth, stretches far out into the sapphire sea; near at hand rises the Piton de la Rivière Noire, the loftiest summit in the island, two thousand five hundred and sixty-four feet. In another direction are visible the green tops of the Tamarin and the Rempart; and in a fourth, the three-headed mountain called the Trois Mamelles. Contiguous to these opens a deep caldron, two of the sides of which have broken down in ruin, while the others remain erect and steep. Besides these mountains, the traveller sees the Corps de Garde du Port Loris de Mocca; Le Pouce, with its narrow peak projecting above the plateau like a thumb; and the precipitous Peter Botte.

The last-named mountain recalls the memory of the daring Hollander who first reached its summit, long regarded as impracticable. He succeeded in what seemed a hopeless effort by shooting an arrow, to which a strong cord was attached, over the top. The arrow fell on the other side of the mountain, at a point which could be attained without much difficulty. A stout rope was then fastened to the cord, drawn over the mountain, and secured on both sides; and Peter Botte hauled himself up by it to the topmost crest, and thus immortalized his name. The ascent has since been accomplished by English travellers.

A trip was also undertaken to the Trou de Cerf, or "Stag's Hole," a crater of perfectly regular formation, brimful of bloom and foliage. As no sign or mark betrays its whereabouts, the traveller is seized with astonishment on suddenly reaching its brink. His astonishment soon wears off, and he feels an intense delight in contemplating the view before him. It comprises three-fourths of the island: majestic mountains clothed in virgin forests almost to their very crests; wide-spreading plains, green with the leafiness of the sugar-cane plantations; cool verdurous valleys, where the drowsy shadows softly rest; and beyond and around the blue sea with a fringe of snow-white foam marking the indentations of the coast.

* * * * *

On the 25th of April 1857 Madame Pfeiffer sailed for Madagascar, and after a six-days' voyage reached the harbour of Tamatavé.

Madagascar, the reader may be reminded, is, next to Borneo, the largest island in the world. It is separated from the African mainland by the Mozambique Channel, only seventy-five miles wide. It stretches from lat. 12° to 25° S., and long. 40° to 48° E. Its area is about ten thousand geographical square miles.

THE TRAVELLER'S TREE.

Madagascar contains forests of immense extent, far-reaching plains and valleys, rivers, lakes, and great chains of mountains, which raise their summits to an elevation of ten or twelve thousand feet. The climate is tropical, the vegetation remarkable for abundance and variety. The chief products are gums and odoriferous balsams, sugar, tobacco, maize, indigo, silk, spices. The woods yield many valuable kinds of timber, and almost every fruit of the Torrid Zone, besides the curious and useful Traveller's Tree. Palms are found in dense and beautiful groves; and among them is the exquisite water-palm, or lattice leaf-plant. In the animal kingdom Madagascar possesses some remarkable forms; as, for instance, the makis, or half-ape, and the black parrot. The population consists of four distinct races: the Kaffirs, who inhabit the south; the Negroes, who dwell in the west; the Arabs in the east; and in the interior the Malays, among whom the Hovas are the most numerous and the most civilized.

* * * * *

Tamatavé, when visited by Madame Pfeiffer looked like a poor but very large village, with between four and five thousand inhabitants. Of late years, however, it has grown into a place of much commercial importance. There are some decent houses; but the natives live chiefly in small huts, which are scattered over a wide area, with scarcely any attempt at regularity of arrangement. These huts are supported on piles from six to ten feet high. They are built of wood or of bamboo, thatched with long grass or palm-leaves; and they contain only one room, of which the fireplace occupies a disproportionate share. Windows are wanting, but light and air are admitted through two opposite doors.

The bazaar is situated in the middle of the village, on an irregular piece of ground, and is distinguished alike by its dirt and poverty. The articles exposed for sale are only a supply of beef, some sugar-cane, rice, and a few fruits; and the whole stock of one of the dealers would be dear at a couple of shillings. The oxen are slaughtered on the spot, and their flesh sold in thick hunches, with the skin, which is esteemed a great delicacy. Meat is not bought according to weight, but the size of each piece is measured by the eye.

The Tamatavians are principally Malagasys; and, physically, their appearance does not recommend them. They have wide mouths, with thick lips; their noses are broad and flat; their chins protrude; their cheek-bones are disagreeably prominent. Their complexion may be any shade of a muddy brown. Generally, their teeth are regular, and very white; but against this redeeming trait must be put their hideous hair, which is coal-black, very long, very woolly, and very coarse. When worn in all its natural amplitude, its effect is curiously disagreeable. The face seems lost in a "boundless convexity" of thick frizzled hair, which stands out in every direction. But, usually, the men cut their hair quite short at the back of the head, leaving only a length of six or eight inches in front, which stands upright, like a hedge of wool. Much pride is felt in their "head of hair" by the women, and even by some of the men; and, unwilling to shorten so ornamental an appendage, they plait it into numerous little tails. Some coquettishly allow these tails to droop all about their head; others twist them together into a band or bunch, covering the top of the head like a cap. No wonder that much time is spent in the preparation of so complex a head-gear; but then, on the other hand, when once made up it will last for several days.

Now as to the costume of these interesting semi-savages. Their articles of clothing are two in number—the *sadik* and the *simbre*. The former, which by many natives is considered quite sufficient, is a strip of cloth worn round the loins. The simbre is a piece of white stuff, about four yards long and three broad, which is worn much like a toga. As it is constantly coming loose, and every minute needing adjustment, it is an exceedingly troublesome though not ungraceful garment, keeping one hand of the wearer almost constantly employed.

Males and females wear the same attire, except that the latter indulge in a little more drapery, and often add a third article—a short tight jacket, called *kanezu*.

Simple as is the clothing of the Malagasy, their food is not less simple. At every meal, rice and anana are the principal or only dishes. Anana is a vegetable very much like spinach, of a by no means disagreeable flavour in itself, but not savoury when cooked with rancid fat. Fish is sometimes eaten, but not often—for indolence is a great Malagasy quality—by those who dwell on the borders of rivers or on the sea-shore; meat and poultry, though both are cheap, are eaten only on special occasions. The natives partake of two meals—one in the morning, the other in the evening.

The rice and anana are washed down with *ranugang*, or rice-water, thus prepared: Rice is boiled in a vessel, and purposely burned, until a crust forms at the bottom. The water is poured on, and allowed to boil. The water in colour resembles pale coffee, and in taste is abominable to a European palate. The natives, however, esteem it highly, and not only drink the water, but eat the crust.

* * * * *

One of the great ceremonies of Madagascar, the royal bath-feast, is described by Madame Pfeiffer. It is celebrated on the Malagasy New-Year's Day, and has some curious features. On the eve, all the high officers, nobles, and chiefs are invited to court; and assembling in a great hall, partake of a dish of rice, which is handed round to each guest with much solemnity that he may take a pinch with his fingers and eat. Next day, all reassemble in the same place; and the queen steps behind a curtain, which hangs in a corner of the room, undresses, and submits to copious ablutions. Assuming her clothes, she comes forward, holding in her hand an ox-horn that has been filled with water from her bath; and this she sprinkles over the assembled company—reserving a portion for the soldiers drawn up on parade beneath her window.

Throughout the country this day is an occasion of festivity, and dancing, singing, and feasting are kept up till a late hour. Nor does the revel end then; it is prolonged for eight days. The people on the first day are accustomed to kill as many oxen as will supply them with meat for the whole period; and no man who possesses a herd, however small, fails to kill at least one for this annual celebration. The poor exchange rice, and tobacco, and several potatoes, for pieces of meat. These pieces are long thin strips; and being salted, and laid one upon another, they keep tolerably well until the eighth day.

Madame Pfeiffer had an opportunity of witnessing the dances, but did not find them very interesting.

Some girls beat a little stick with all their might against a thick stem of bamboo; while others sang, or rather howled, at their highest and loudest pitch. Then two of the ebony beauties stepped forward, and began to move slowly to and fro on a small space of ground, half lifting their arms, and turning their hands, first outwards, and then towards their sides. Next, one of the men made his *début*. He tripped about much in the same style as the dusky *danseuses*, only with greater energy; and each time he approached any of the women or girls, he made gestures expressive of his love and admiration.

* * * * *

Our traveller obtained permission to enter into the interior of the island, and to visit Antananarivo, {197} the capital. As she approached it, she could see it picturesquely planted on a high hill that rose out of the broad and fertile inland plain; and after a pleasant journey through rich and beautiful scenery, she came upon the suburbs, which enclose it on all sides.

The suburbs at first were villages; but they have gradually expanded until they have been formed into a compact aggregate. Most of the houses are built of earth or clay; but those belonging to the city must, by royal decree, be constructed of planks, or at least of bamboo. They are all of a larger size than the dwellings of the villagers; are much cleaner, and kept in better condition. The roofs are very high and steep, with long poles reared at each end by way of ornament. Many houses, and sometimes groups of three or four houses, are surrounded by low ramparts of earth, apparently for no other purpose than to separate the courtyards from the neighbouring tenements. The streets and squares are all very irregularly built: the houses are not placed in rows, but in clusters,—some at the foot of the hill, others on its slopes. The royal palace crowns the summit.

Madame Pfeiffer expressing her surprise at the number of lightning-conductors that everywhere appeared, was informed that perhaps in no other part of the world were thunderstorms so frequent or so fatal. She was told that, at Antananarivo, about three hundred people were killed by lightning every year.

The interior of the town was in appearance exactly like one of the suburbs, except that the houses were built of planks or of bamboo.

At the time of Madame Pfeiffer's visit, the sovereign of Madagascar was Queen Ranavala, memorable for her sanguinary propensities, her hatred of Europeans, and her persecution of the Christian converts. It proves the extraordinary power of fascination which our traveller possessed, that she obtained from this feminine despot so many concessions—being allowed to travel about the island with comparative freedom, and being even admitted to the royal presence. The latter incident is thus described:—

Towards four o'clock in the afternoon her bearers carried Madame Pfeiffer to the palace, over the door of which a great gilded eagle expands its wings. According to rule, in stepping across the threshold the visitor put her right foot foremost; and this ceremony she also observed on entering, through a second gateway, the spacious courtyard in front of the palace. Here the queen was visible, being seated on a balcony on the first story, and Madame Pfeiffer and her attendants were directed to stand in a row in the courtyard opposite to her. Under the balcony some soldiers were going through divers evolutions, which concluded, comically enough, by suddenly lifting up the right foot as if it had been stung by a wasp.

The queen was attired in a wide silk simbre, and wore on her head a large golden crown. Though she sat in the shade, a very ample umbrella of crimson silk—throughout the East a sign of royal dignity—was held over her head. She was of rather dark complexion, strongly and even sturdily built, and, though seventy-five years of age, remarkably healthy and active. On her right stood her son, Prince Rakoto; and on her left, her adopted son, Prince Ramboasalama. Behind her were gathered nephews, nieces, and other relatives, and the dignitaries and grandees of her kingdom.

The minister who had conducted Madame Pfeiffer and her companion—M. Lambert, a French adventurer, who played a conspicuous part in the affairs of Madagascar—addressed a short speech to the queen; after which the visitors had to bow thrice, and to repeat the words, "Esaratsara tombokoc" (We salute you cordially); to which she replied, "Esaratsara" (We salute you). They then turned to the left to salute King Radama's tomb, which was close at hand, with three similar bows; afterwards returning to their former position in front of the balcony, and making three more. M. Lambert next held up a gold piece of eighty francs value, and placed it in the hands of the minister who had introduced them. This gift, which is expected from every stranger when first presented, is called "Monosina." The queen then asked M. Lambert if he wished to put any question to her, or if he needed anything, and also addressed a remark or two to Madame Pfeiffer. The bowings and greetings were then resumed; obeisance was paid to King Radama's monument; and the visitors, as they retired, were again cautioned not to put the left foot first over the threshold.

The royal palace is (or was) a very large timber building, consisting of a ground-floor and two stories, surmounted by a singularly high-pitched roof. Each story is surrounded by a broad gallery. The roof is supported on wooden pillars, eighty feet high, and rises forty feet above them, resting in the centre on a pillar not less than a hundred and twenty feet in height. All these columns are fashioned each from a single trunk; and when it is considered, says our authority, that the forests containing trees of sufficient size for this purpose lie fifty or sixty miles from the capital, that the roads are nowhere paved, and in some places are quite impassable, and that all the pillars are dragged to the capital without the help of a beast of burden or any single machine, and are afterwards wrought and set up with the simplest tools, the erection of this palace may justly be called a gigantic undertaking, and the palace itself ranked among the wonders of the world.

The government of Madagascar has always been Draconian in its severity, and the penalty exacted for almost every offence is blood. Some of the unfortunates are burned; others are hurled over a high rock; others buried alive; others scalded to death with boiling water; others killed with the spear; others sewn up alive in mats, and left to perish of hunger and corruption; and others beheaded. Recourse is not unfrequently had to poison, which is used as a kind of ordeal or test. This is applicable to all classes; and as any one may accuse another, on depositing a certain sum of money,—and as, moreover, no accused person is allowed to defend himself,—the ordeal does not fall into disrepute for want of use. If the accused endures it without perishing, a third part of the deposit is awarded to him, a third part goes to the court, and the remainder is returned to the accuser. But if the accused die, his guilt is considered to have been established, and the accuser receives back the whole of his money.

The poisoning process takes place as follows:—

The material employed is obtained from the kernel of a fruit as large as a peach, called the *Tanghinia venenifera*. The lampi-tanghini, or person who administers the poison, announces to the accused the day on which the perilous dose is to be swallowed. For eight-and-forty hours before the prescribed time he is allowed to eat very little, and for the last twenty-four hours nothing at all. His friends accompany him to the poisoner's house. There he undresses, and takes oath that he has had no recourse to magic. The lampi-tanghini then scrapes away as much powder from the kernel with a knife as he judges necessary for the trial. Before administering the dose, he asks the accused if he confesses his crime; which the accused never does, because under any circumstances he would have to swallow the poison. The said poison is spread upon three little pieces of skin, each about an inch in size, cut from the back of a plump fowl. These he rolls together, and administers to the supposed culprit.

"In former days," says Madame Pfeiffer, "almost every person who was subjected to this ordeal died in great agony; but for the last ten years any one not condemned by the queen herself to take the tanghin, is allowed to make use of the following antidote. As soon as he has taken the poison, his friends make him drink rice-water in such quantities that his whole body sometimes swells visibly, and quick and violent vomiting is brought on. If the poisoned man be fortunate enough to get rid not only of the poison, but of the three little skins (which latter must be returned uninjured), he is declared innocent, and his relations carry him home in triumph, with songs and rejoicings. But if one of the pieces of skin should fail to reappear, or if it be at all injured, his life is forfeited, and he is executed with the spear, or by some other means." {204}

* * * * *

During Madame Pfeiffer's stay at Antananarivo a conspiracy broke out, provoked by the queen's cruelty. It failed, however, in its object; and those concerned in it were mercilessly punished. The Christians became anew exposed to the suspicions and wrath of Ranavala; and Madame Pfeiffer and her companions found themselves in a position of great peril. The royal council debated vehemently the question, Whether they should be put to death? and this being answered in the affirmative, What death they should die? Happily, Prince Rakoto interfered, pointing out that the murder of Europeans would not be allowed to pass unavenged, but would bring down upon Madagascar the fleets and armies of the great European powers. This argument finally prevailed; and Madame Pfeiffer and the other Europeans, six in all, then in Antananarivo, were ordered to quit it immediately. They were only too thankful to escape with their lives, and within an hour were on their way to Tamatavé, escorted by seventy Malagasy soldiers. They had good cause to congratulate themselves on their escape, for on the very morning of their departure ten Christians had been put to death with the most terrible tortures.

The journey to Tamatavé was not without its dangers and difficulties, and Madame Pfeiffer, who had been attacked with fever, suffered severely. The escort purposely delayed them on the road; so that, instead of reaching the coast in eight days, the time actually occupied was three-and-fifty. This was the more serious, because the road ran through low-lying and malarious districts. In the most unhealthy spots, moreover, the travellers were left in wretched huts for a whole week, or even two weeks; and frequently, when Madame Pfeiffer was groaning in a violent excess of fever, the brutal soldiers dragged her from her miserable couch, and compelled her to continue her journey.

At length, on the 12th of September, she arrived at Tamatavé; broken-down and unutterably weary and worn, but still alive. Ill as she was, she gladly embarked on board a ship which was about to sail for the Mauritius;

and reaching that pleasant island on the 22nd, met with a hearty welcome from her friends—to whom, indeed, she was as one who had been dead and was alive again.

The mental and physical sufferings she had undergone, combined with the peculiar effects of the fever, now brought on an illness of so serious a character that for long the doctors doubted whether her recovery was possible. On her sixtieth birthday, the 14th of October, they pronounced the brave lady out of danger; but, in fact, her constitution had received a fatal shock. The fever became intermittent in its attacks, but it never wholly left her; though she continued, with unabated energy and liveliness, to lay down plans for fresh expeditions. She had made all her preparations for a voyage to Australia, when a return of her disease, in February 1858, compelled her to renounce her intention, and to direct her steps homeward.

Early in the month of June she arrived in London, where she remained for a few weeks. Thence she repaired to Berlin.

Her strength was now declining day by day, though at first she seemed to regard her illness as only temporary, and against the increasing physical weakness her mind struggled with its usual activity. About September, she evinced a keen anxiety to behold her home once more,—evidently having arrived at a conviction that her end was near. She was carefully conveyed to Vienna, and received into the house of her brother, Charles Reyer; where, at first, the influence of her native air had an invigorating effect. This gave way after a week or two, and her illness returned with augmented force. During the last days of her life, opiates were administered to relieve her sufferings; and in the night between the 27th and 28th of October she passed away peacefully, and apparently without pain,—leaving behind her the memory of a woman of matchless intrepidity, surprising energy, and heroic fixity of purpose.

NOTES.

{105} Since Madame Pfeiffer's time this mode of self-torture has been prohibited by the British Government.

{197} That is, the "City of a Thousand Towns."

{204} We give Madame Pfeiffer's account, as an illustration of the old ways of Madagascar society. But the poison-ordeal has of late been abandoned, owing to Christian influence.

Milton Keynes UK
Ingram Content Group UK Ltd.
UKHW042146281024
450365UK00010B/651